Ron Heyn

A Better Way

JONES MEDIA
PUBLISHING

A Better Way
Ron Heyn

Jones Media Publishing
10645 N. Tatum Blvd. Ste. 200-166
Phoenix, AZ 85028
www.JonesMediaPublishing.com

Printed in the United States of America

ISBN-13: 978-1-945849-42-8

First Edition March 2017
10 9 8 7 6 5 4 3 2 1

Contents

Introduction

Years ago my wife and I were asked to speak at a convention on the subject of forgiveness. When we did speak, people apparently experienced healing in their lives. Out of that we began praying for people and most of the time they were healed. It was out of this experience that this book emerged.

I have written this book based on my personal experiences. I am not an expert in theology, nor do I consider myself to be a Scripture scholar. Rather I have come to know that I am a child of God and, that, over the years, God's love has touched me deeply. I am bursting to share my experience of His love with others.

I would ask you to read this book from a window of your own life's experiences and to allow God's love to touch your heart as you read. My wife and I have given many talks sharing our joys and our heartaches in life, but always with the intent of sharing how God moved in each situation. We have learned that while sharing how God moves, most people are encouraged. However, occasionally, someone will approach us with a comment like "I am sorry you had so much trouble in your family." That person has missed the point. Life can be messy. I don't think any person or family is exempt from the messes in life. I believe we all can use a deeper touch from God. This book hopefully invites you into a deeper relationship with our God to help deal with the messes life brings us.

One of the things I hope to address is some misconceptions we have about God, especially with regard to healing. I learned over the years that I cannot put God in the box I have created in my mind for Him. I have to move beyond my own life experience to define my understanding of God. Instead, I have attempted to get my answers from the Bible, the Word of God. After all, it tells us in the Gospel of John (read John 1:1-15) that Jesus is the Word of God made flesh. In fact there is so much in those verses; one could spend a long time drinking in its meaning.

Let me tell one story of how I have kept God in my own little box for many years. When I have been asked to lay hands on someone I have always prayed for the person's healing. I believe God wants us healed. In the book of Ecclesiastes, in the third chapter, it tells us there is a time for everything, including a time to die. One evening we were having dinner with a friend when she got a call asking her to come to Hospice where a close friend of hers was dying from cancer. We went with her and we were invited to pray over her. I started to pray for healing, as I always do, when suddenly I found myself reciting the 23rd Psalm. When I finished I knew she was going to die and that it was "her time to die." When she did not die that evening, nor did she die the next day, I began to wonder (are you ready for this?) if I left out some of the words from the Psalm. I immediately stopped myself from that kind of foolish thinking. The next day she did die. During my prayer time I heard the Spirit of God say to me, "Thank you for being my voice. She needed to audibly hear those words in order to let go and come home to me." I thought wow, I just cannot keep holding onto my view of God and His intentions. Instead, I experienced yet another time when I realized I needed to yield my thoughts to His thoughts in order to hear His heart.

When I listen to a speaker or read a book I sometimes think this would really be good for so-and-so to hear or to read. I would ask you to read this for yourself and when you are finished, if you are so moved, then tell the other person about it. I believe that you will be blessed and perhaps understand just a little bit more the height and depth of God's love for you….and that maybe, if He's been in your box of understanding, you too can expand your view of Him in your life.

Enjoy.

Acknowledgements

I would like to thank a host of people who have helped me with this book. Before I do that I need to say I had a list of people on my computer so that I would not forget anyone but one day the computer went down and I did not have that file saved. So forgive me if you read this and I did not include you in my acknowledgements.

First I need to thank my wife Anita for being a sounding board and for correcting my grammar etc. I need to add my friend Tom Schissel who has graciously labored reading my various drafts, for giving my input on what to include and how to express it. I also need to thank Brenda Theilen for her sharp eye in finding many of the mistakes that needed correction. I also want to thank Barbara Regnier for taking the time to read my book and giving me insightful views of what I had included. Finally, I want to thank Jimmy Keane for taking the time to not only read the book but for giving me very insightful suggestions on how and where to express some of my ideas.

I would be remiss if I did not thank Kathy McGuire and Hazel Greenfield for their words of encouragement to continue the project.

The cover art of the book was created by my grandson, Danny Fischetti. I thank him for doing the cover while playing baseball on his high school team, while finishing his studies during his senior year and while applying to colleges to continue his studies.

I also need to thank Deb Ravin for taking Danny's drawing and putting it into a form that could be submitted to the publishing company. Deb also made many corrections to my grammar and she pointed many areas where I needed to take a close look at how I had expressed my ideas. In some cases she correctly suggested I either delete something or rewrite it. For this I am very grateful.

Chapter 1

The Phone Call

It was Friday when the phone rang at around 3:00 in the morning. I was in a very deep sleep. I know this because the phone started to ring from what sounded like a great distance away and with each ring it got closer and louder. Finally, when my wife, Anita, poked me to answer it I reached over and picked up the receiver. The voice on the other end asked "Mr. Heyn?" I said yes and the person said this is "Mary, Mary Nuesca, Linda's roommate." Our daughter, Linda, was a 19 year old sophomore at the University of San Diego, a small Catholic University located in California. We lived in Phoenix. Mary went on to tell me that Linda had been in an accident. Actually she had been attacked by a man and thrown off the Marina Street bridge and had fallen some 27 feet in to a dry river bed. Mary went on to tell me that Linda had broken her leg and had hurt her back and that she was in the hospital. I had trouble comprehending everything she was saying. I don't know if it was because I was still half asleep or if I was in denial of what I was hearing. I was still in recovery from deep depression and my psyche may have instinctively been protecting me from the reality of this shocking and disturbing news. In any case I thanked Mary for calling and hung up the phone. When I got off the phone, Anita asked me who had called. I told her that Mary, Linda's roommate had called and that Linda was in an accident and was in the hospital.

Anita asked "Is she all right?" "I don't know" was my reply. What hospital is she in? "I don't know." My head was swirling and everything was like a huge fog. "What are we going to do," she asked? "I don't know! Please give me a chance to think!" I had never been so disoriented in my life. Normally I rise to the occasion when there is any kind of a crisis. I consider myself to be a take charge kind of guy. At this very moment I felt helpless. I closed my eyes and started to pray. My college roommate came to mind. Ken is a medical doctor who was on the faculty at the University of California San Diego. He had been one of the ushers at our wedding 21 years earlier and we had kept in close touch over the years. I opened my eyes and told Anita I would call Ken. "At 3:00 in the morning?" she asked. "Yes, I'll call now," I told her.

We looked up his number and I dialed it very carefully, not wanting to awaken some stranger by dialing the wrong number. When Ken answered he was very groggy and I will never forget the change that took place in his demeanor when I told him who it was and that Linda had been in some sort of an accident. Ken went from that very groggy person answering the phone at 3:00 A.M. to the trained medical professional, alert and very clinical in nature. "Exactly where did the accident occur?" "Was she taken to a hospital?" "Just what exactly do you want me to do for you?" I told him I had failed to get the name of the hospital and had no telephone number to call to get more information. He told me to hang up and wait by the phone and he would call back in a few minutes.

Anita and I sat there for what seemed like an eternity waiting for the phone to ring. We decided we needed to pray. I told her I needed to pray as I was afraid I might go off the deep end emotionally. I can honestly say that for the first time in my life I really needed God, that I could not handle the situation. I just couldn't deal with everything that was happening. As I started to pray I had what I will call a vision. In my mind's eye, I saw Jesus standing before this man. I knew it was the man who had attacked Linda. Jesus said to the man, "You are very hurting, if you come to me I will heal you." I became flooded with compassion for the man and the vision disappeared. I knew that without doubt we needed to pray for him as well as for Linda.

A couple of minutes later the phone rang. Ken had all the information. He had located the hospital and gotten the phone number to reach Mary etc. He offered us a place to stay and a car to drive. He gave me his office number and said he would be available for whatever we might need. We thanked him and hung up.

We called the hospital and located Mary, this time with Anita on the phone. We got more information about Linda's condition. Mary also gave us several numbers to reach her and told us she would meet us at the airport once we had made arrangements.

The next thing we did was place a call to Southwest Airlines and made plane reservations to San Diego. About 4:00 A.M. we called Father Mike Conley, C.S.C, a Holy Cross priest with whom we were working in our leadership position in the World Wide Marriage Encounter movement. We told Mike what had happened to Linda and asked him to pray for Linda and for the man who had attacked her. He offered to come right over but we said we would only be getting ready to leave and asked that he call various people on the board we served on and in the Phoenix Marriage Encounter community to ask them to pray for both Linda and the man who attacked her.

We realized we had time to go to the morning Mass at our parish. We woke our other three children and told them what had happened and asked them to go to Mass with us. When we got to the church we were early enough to go in and ask the priest to pray and to announce to the community what had happened, asking for prayers for both Linda and the man who attacked her.

We were blessed to be attending a parish that had a grade school associated with it and we were very blessed to have about 10 to 12 nuns in residence at the parish and working at the school. When Mass ended, Sister Raphael Quinn, the school principal rushed up to tell us how sorry she was and that the entire community of nuns would be praying as would the entire school. We realized that something this outrageous did get the attention of people. We also believed it got them to pray.

We got home and I called my boss's home and reached his wife. We asked her to tell him that I would not be at work that day. She came right over with her two school aged children and asked if there was any way she could help. We asked her to pray. She then informed us that my boss, her husband, had left her for another woman, but that she would inform him as to what happened and that she and the children would pray. She also indicated she would call others from her church and have them pray. They were of another faith and despite the pain in her own life she rose above it to reach out to our hurting family. We were only beginning to experience the incredible power of the Christian community around us.

Anita's mother who lived a few miles away was a late sleeper but we had to call her to be at our house when the children arrived home from school and to stay with them for the weekend. I don't know if she comprehended all that we told her but in her great goodness she assured us she would be there.

We also called our closest friends, Bill and Karen, from the Church and the Marriage Encounter and asked Karen to pick up our son Christopher from school when he got out and to look after Nana and the children while we were gone. We also asked them and their family to pray.

We then headed for the airport. While walking through the airport we spotted a nun wearing her habit. We stopped her and told her what had happened and asked her to pray for Linda and the man who had attacked her. She told us she was from Oregon and the sixty or so nuns would be praying as soon as she got back to her community.

We boarded the plane and as it took off Anita started to read. I was too shook up to read so for the entire hour or so of the flight I sang the words "Praise God" to the tune of Amazing Grace quietly to myself. By the time we landed in San Diego my spirit and my emotions had quieted down and as we walked off the plane I knew deep inside that everything would be all right. Our daughter's roommate, Mary met us at the gate (this was before 9/11) and I asked her if Linda's face had been beaten. Why I asked that question I don't know. She assured me her face was fine. After that I don't remember much of the conversation as she drove us to the hospital to see Linda. I think I spent most of that time praying.

When we got to Linda's room she was not in her bed, she was in a wheel chair and down the hall visiting and ministering to other patients. When we caught up to her she said some of the other patients were far worse than she was and she just wanted to help them any way she could.

Later that day the orthopedic surgeon who was brought in to examine Linda came to her room and told us she had a broken leg and had crushed five vertebrae in her lower back. He told us he did not see how she would ever walk again. I told myself this was not what God wanted for her.

Let me digress for a moment to interject an important fact in the story. The weekend before this happened we, her mother and I, had taken her car away from her because we judged she had been irresponsible in its use and in its upkeep. Consequently, early on the Thursday evening after we had taken the car away, Linda was walking home from an off campus job when this horrendous event occurred. Linda told us she was crossing the Marina Street Bridge when a man approached her and tried to abduct her. She fought with him and he picked her up and threw her off the bridge where she fell 27 feet into the dry river bed. She said she clung to the railing of the bridge and he, the assailant, removed her hands so she would fall. She said she gave her life to God as she fell and she said it was an almost joy filled fall as she was sure she was going home to the Lord. When she hit the ground this sense of joy and peace left her as she experienced a tremendous amount of physical pain. She said that for an instant she was angry that she had not died, but reality set in quickly as she now had to survive. On impact she broke her leg, crushed five vertebrae in her lower back, chipped her teeth and everything in between seemed to hurt. When the man saw that she was alive, he went down into the river bed to rape her. She talked him out of that but he did some other horrible things to her and then took her driver's license and threatened to kill her if she told anyone. He left her there and she waited about 30 minutes and then proceeded to crawl out of the river bed on her elbows singing songs she had sung at Young Life and at other youth retreats she had attended through the church. She lay on the sidewalk in the dark until someone came along to help her.

The police apparently had sent 32 units into the area looking for the man that attacked Linda. Based on the description Linda had given them one of the police officers came upon the man just as he was heading back to his normal area of patrol. When he stopped to talk to the suspect, the man said, "If this is about that girl near Presidio Park, I had nothing to do with it." When they looked in his backpack, they found Linda's driver's license.

Chapter 2

Our Background

I think it is appropriate I tell you a little bit about our backgrounds and what our life had been like leading up to this point. I do this with the intention of pointing out that we are just ordinary people. I hope this book will lead to an understanding that God wants to be a working part of all of our lives. We discovered that we just have to let Him in.

Anita and I were both born in the same year, 1938, only 27 days apart. Anita was born into an Italian Catholic family that was living in Brooklyn, New York. I was born into a family of German descent. My family attended the Lutheran Church. I was born in Mineola, New York and spent the first 11 years of my life living in a town called Stewart Manor which is on Long Island. Anita's father was a lawyer, mine was a factory worker. Neither of my parents were educated past the eighth grade. My father had learned his trade in Germany as a blacksmith. At age eighteen he had boarded a ship for the United States and never saw his parents again. My mother came to the U.S. as a baby so she never really learned German.

Growing up our lives revolved around family, and in my case it included the extended family from my mother's side, and also around church activities. My mother was religious but my father was not. He attended church basically on Easter and on Christmas Eve. I am sure he went to church at other times, but it was not very often. I remember attending Sunday school and church each Sunday. It was during this time that I began to believe the stories in the Bible, particularly those that talked about Jesus and His life. Our social life was basically with other people of German descent. During World War II my father worked at an airplane factory where he built the first models of the P-47 Thunderbolt. We didn't see a lot of him during this period as he was working what seemed like day and night.

Anita's life was also church and family centered. She and her sister attended a private Catholic grade school that was strictly for girls. The school was run by cloistered nuns who never came out in public. Only the children went in to the convent/school grounds. The parents visited with the nuns through screens. It was at this school where Anita's faith was formed. During the war Anita's dad worked in the Brooklyn Naval Yard at night helping to build ships in addition to practicing law during the day.

When I was 11 years old my parents decided to buy a dairy farm in upstate New York. The farm they bought was located halfway between Cooperstown and Cherry Valley. My brother and I attended Cherry Valley Central School at the advice of our real estate agent. Shortly after we moved there my parents ran out of money and we were very close to losing the farm and becoming homeless. My mother insisted that my dad take her to church to pray as she never learned to drive. After a big fight about it, he gave in and took us all to church. My mother said she prayed that day for a job and the next day she found a job. It probably prevented us from being in the street. I was confirmed in that Lutheran Church we attended, at age 13, and never went to church again until after I had met Anita. My mother had given me a wallet sized picture of Christ which had the caption under it that read, "I am with you always." I carried that picture in my wallet and from time to time would take it out and look at it. While looking at it I would think I am just not worthy of being His follower and I would put the picture back in my wallet.

Aside from working on the farm, my life revolved around school and more specifically basketball. I played three sports in high school: football, basketball and baseball, but basketball was my sport. I grew to be 6 feet 6 inches tall, which was huge for those days, and I played on a team that did not lose many games. My senior year I was selected as captain of the team. We went through the season undefeated and I was the leading scorer with 15.5 points per game. We had six kids in double figures and our coach would not let us run up any scores. I was recruited by a number of colleges but I had my heart set on going to Colgate, the school where we played our tournament games at the end of each season. I told the coach that my parents had no money to send me to school and that meant I needed a full scholarship: room board, tuition and books. We discussed the subject and he told me that in order to award that kind of scholarship, I would need to agree to play football as well as basketball. I decided that playing football at the college level was not for me, so I turned down the offer. I ended up starting to work for the General Electric Company on a training program where I was to attend Union College in Schenectady, New York at night while working full time.

That summer the family which bought our house on Long Island six years earlier came up to visit. They had a daughter who was entering her senior year in high school. We started to write to each other and she invited me to take her out on a date on Saturday evening of Labor Day weekend. I accepted, and on Saturday of that weekend I was in my god father's grocery store on Long Island. A man from the nearby sporting goods store came in. During the conversation my god father told him that I was a good basketball player. When he realized I was not going to college to play ball he asked me if I would be interested in playing for Adelphi College. I jumped at the idea and he called the athletic director and basketball coach. Upon hearing that I was 6 feet 6 inches tall he came right over to see me. To make a long story short I got a scholarship to Adelphi.

During Anita's high school years, she and her family spent 18 months living in Cuba, before the Castro regime. They were there with another family investing in an import business. Her dad continued with his law practice in Brooklyn and commuted to Cuba once a month or so. In the 18 months in Cuba, Anita became fluent in Spanish. In the US she attended Packer Collegiate Institute a college prep school for girls. Anita was an honor student and she had her eyes on some of the more exclusive girls' colleges in the Northeast. The family had moved to Garden City which happened to be where Adelphi College (now University) was located. Her father asked her to go to school locally as he was not sure he could afford the more prestigious schools she had aspired to attend. Reluctantly she accepted his request.

During the orientation week for freshmen, they brought several groups of us into the library to learn how to use the library. Anita was in one of the other groups. I cannot remember being so enchanted by a girl. I spent the entire library orientation staring at her. I decided I was going to date her. I didn't see her again the rest of orientation week but when I was sitting in speech class on Monday morning she came into the room. She was late, because the professor from her previous class always kept the students overtime. When she sat in the back of the class I promptly got up and moved to the back of the room to sit next to her. The professor asked me if I was settled and I assured her that I was.

I wasted no time after that class to introduce myself to Anita and to ask her to attend a dance that was put on for the freshmen to meet each other. The dance was to be on Saturday evening in the school gym. It was called the "Howdy Hop." As quickly as I asked her, Anita turned me down, stating that it would be a good time to meet lots of people and that she would see me there. I didn't know if this was some slick city girl politely blowing off the hayseed or not, but I really did not have a choice.

When the night of the dance came, Anita's mother would not allow her to attend the dance without her older brother escorting her (part of the Italian culture.) He brought along several of his friends, all of whom were also Italian. With no joking intended, from a distance I thought she was with some guy who looked Italian to me, so I figured she had simply blown me off. I did not approach her that evening and I went home very disappointed. After class on Monday Anita asked me where I had been. She said she had looked for me and was disappointed that we didn't meet up. I didn't know if I really believed her, but if you know Anita, even now, she had and has such a beautiful welcoming smile that I finally bought her story about her brother and his friends. Although to this day I still believe one of his friends was hitting on her. She was, I believe, naïve enough to not even realize it.

A few weeks later I asked her to go to the "All College Ball", a formal dance for all students and their dates. The dance was being held at a country club on the North Shore of Long Island, so one needed a car to get there. I had arranged a double date with another guy who had a car. When she said yes, one of my aunts helped me to get a tuxedo rental and arrange for me to buy flowers. Between the dance tickets, the tuxedo and the flowers, I don't even know how I paid for them. I think I skipped quite a few meals. The day of the dance, my friend sought me out to tell me his date was sick and that they wouldn't be going to the dance. I was crushed as I had no way to get Anita to the dance. I found Anita on campus and told her my dilemma and offered her the tickets, flowers etc. She called her mother from the library and her mother agreed to allow us to use their family car. I then had to call another aunt who later drove twenty some miles to pick me up at the house where I was living (there were no men's dorms at the school) and drive me to Anita's house some three miles away. I met her parents and then we left for the dance.

We both loved to dance and had a wonderful evening. We had our picture taken and I bought the pictures for us to have. When I drove her home and we were approaching the steps of her house I wanted to ask her if I could kiss her. Instead she asked me if I wanted to come in for something to eat. I was a starving basketball player and I don't think I had eaten dinner that night as I had neither the time nor the money. I jumped at the idea. Anita brought donuts and milk to the family room where we were talking and in the middle of all of it, she kissed me. I can only tell you I danced all the way home as I walked the three miles back to the house where I was living.

We dated for the four years we attended college, I asked her to marry me in our senior year and we were married in her Catholic Church shortly before we both began our teaching jobs.

We eventually moved to Phoenix, Arizona where we believed we could afford a home, something we could not seem to be able to do on Long Island. Our first daughter, Linda, had been born on Long Island. By the time we moved to Phoenix we were pregnant with our second daughter, Lisa. We also had bought our first home shortly after Lisa was born. We were married five years by now. On Labor Day weekend we were painting a crib when a priest, Father Marc Tillia, came to visit. Anita invited him into the house and offered him some iced tea. We sat in the living room when he told us he had come to invite me to attend inquiry classes to see what it would mean for me to join the Catholic Church. He was such a beautiful gentle soul that I could not say no to him. I agreed to attend the classes which were starting the following Monday evening.

When Monday evening came we had a thunderstorm that one might call a gully washer. I was really starting to feel pressure building up inside me with regard to these classes. I really did not want to attend them. I am not sure if I didn't feel worthy, or if I was just too lazy to take on the responsibility. Linda, our oldest was already asking why daddy didn't go to church with them, but here again my self-centeredness took over. I told Anita I wasn't going to the class. I used the thunderstorm as my excuse. Anita got very upset and went into our bedroom and cried for several hours. She seemed inconsolable. After several hours she told me that she had been praying for nine years (the four years we had dated and the five years we were married) that I would join her in her faith. She told me she loved her Catholic faith so much and that she loved me so much that she wanted me to experience what she had. She said she was incomplete without that. I was so moved by the depth of her desires that I assured her I would attend the classes, which I did. I was baptized into the Catholic Church on December 21, 1964. Prior to the baptism we also had our first confession. Father Tillia asked me in the confessional if I wanted his help through the confession, which I did. Every question he asked me made me think he had been following me around all my life, like a guardian angel. I had never felt so cleansed nor as close to God up to that point in my life. That night, as part of this wonderful celebration our third daughter Cathy was conceived. "How do you know that?" you might ask. "I know because I know" is my answer.

During the next few years, Anita stayed pretty busy being a stay at home mom and I got more and more involved in my job as a software developer. In 1969 my boss decided to leave the company and go with a startup company in Pennsylvania. He offered me an opportunity to go with him. Anita liked our life in Phoenix and did not want to go. I really did not give her much of a say in the decision. I had visions of becoming rich from the stock options and pay increase that were being offered as an incentive to join the new company. We moved to Pennsylvania. Within eighteen months the economy had turned downward and we were getting ready to close down the new company. The stock was worthless and it seemed there were no jobs to be had anywhere. About that time I was sitting in my boss's office when he got a phone call from his old boss offering to give him and the five people he had enticed to follow him to Pennsylvania our old jobs back. My boss shocked me when he told the caller that if he wanted him back he had to make an offer to all thirteen people that were working for him. When he hung up the phone I said, "Bill, what are you doing? There are no jobs out there!" Bill was one of the finest Christian men I had ever known. His response to me was "where is your faith? I am a shepherd of my people and I will not abandon them no matter how bad times are."

His response shocked me. Here we were about to be out on the street with no work and he was applying his Christian principles to the situation. It made me look at how I was living out my own Christianity. A week later

Bill was informed that our old company would make job offers to Bill and the thirteen people that were working for him. That included me.

The new job brought us back to Phoenix. I estimated we lost a sizeable amount of money in the eighteen months we were in Pennsylvania, to say nothing about the benefits lost due to the break in service, but the experience in Bills office that day had made a tremendous impression on me which I believed laid the foundation making it all worth the cost.

In 1976 Anita and I were invited by some friends to attend a weekend for marriage, called the Marriage Encounter Weekend. We were both very busy people at the time. Anita was working on her master's degree in Spanish, we had four children by then as our son Christopher had been born in Pennsylvania, and we were avid tennis players. In fact we belonged to two tennis tournament clubs which put us in a tournament at least once a month.

We arrived at the weekend with our tennis rackets in the trunk of the car along with a large cooler filled with beer and the makings of wine coolers. When the weekend got started we realized we would have time for neither tennis nor the refreshments.

On Saturday afternoon of the Marriage Encounter weekend our lives were changed dramatically. After listening to a talk on "God's Plan for Marriage" I was in the conference room writing my reflections on the questions they had given us. Anita was in the room that had been assigned to us, to stay in, doing the same thing. While I was writing deep inside me I heard God say to me "I want you to change your lives." People will often ask if I actually heard his voice with my ears. The answer is no. I can only explain it as hearing His voice deep within my spirit. When the bell rang signaling that we were to head back to our rooms to exchange our reflections with our spouses, I practically ran to the room. I was trying to get the room key in the door when Anita opened the door and excitedly said "I have something I need to tell you". I told her I also had something to tell her but she should go first, thinking that what I had to share would overwhelm both of us. Anita said that while she was writing her reflections that God had told her that He wanted us to change our lives. We just held each other and cried. We knew we would never be the same from that moment on. We wondered what changing our lives meant. We also decided it had to be good, whatever it would be.

At the end of the weekend we were called to the room of one of the team couples who were giving the weekend. When we got there all the team members were there, three couples and the priest. They asked us if we would consider going on what they called a deeper weekend with the intention of possibly joining them in giving future weekends. I said yes, without even hesitating as I assumed this was the beginning of what God wanted from us. They told us we should make the decision together. I looked at Anita and she also said yes. They thanked us and told us someone would get in touch with us with follow up details.

We went home that evening, knowing our lives would never be the same. We were right. We went on the deeper weekend, which was another spiritually powerful experience. After the weekend we wrote talks and gave weekends and within a year or so we were coordinating the Marriage Encounter experience for the western section of the Phoenix Catholic diocese. About a year later we were coordinating a large section of the southwest. Our area included Arizona, Utah, Nevada, part of southern

California and a portion of New Mexico. We also added Father Michael Conley, a priest of the Holy Cross order to our team as coordinators. We were on the go constantly, trying to parent four busy children. I was working full time in the software development field and Anita had returned to teaching Spanish full time.

Chapter 3
Linda's First Healing

In February of 1980, I had what I refer to as a nervous breakdown. I was hospitalized for three weeks and I was out of work for fifteen weeks. When I returned to work I was incapable of performing my job at a satisfactory level. I was, for the first and only time in my life, put on probation at my job.

That summer we celebrated our wedding anniversary at home with Fr. Mike coming to the house to celebrate Mass along with five or six couples that we were close to. Before they all got to our house I had what I will call an anxiety attack. I locked myself in the bed room and would not allow anyone in. They celebrated our anniversary Mass in the living room without me. When I got up in the morning I opened the bedroom door and found love notes from Fr. Mike and each of the couples telling me how much they loved me and that they were praying for me and for both of us. I had such a deep sense of sorrow for my actions that I not only asked Anita for forgiveness, but I wrote a letter to Fr. Mike and to each of the couples asking for forgiveness and for their continued prayers. I believe I had experienced what another priest, Fr. Chuck Gallagher, S.J. had often referred to as compunction. Compunction was defined by him as being a deep sorrow for how our actions (sin) had affected others. This sorrow was not because we are so bad but because the people we often hurt by our actions are so good. Fr. Gallagher tied the need for compunction into the healing process.

The next day Anita was at Mass when some friends

offered some tapes they had recorded on the "healing of memories". The tapes were created at a retreat given by Father John Hampsch, CMF, a Claretian Priest from the Los Angeles area. Our friends told Anita to let them know when we would listen to the tapes so and they could pray for us during that time. The following Saturday night we lay down on our bed to listen to the tapes that ran some three hours. I had such deep healings that I could again begin to perform my work responsibilities.

A week and a half later was when Linda was attacked and we got the phone call mentioned at the beginning of the book.

Linda was released from the hospital in San Diego after a few days and we brought her home to Phoenix. While she got around on crutches, she could not sit up without being propped up by pillows. We even had to help hold her up when she was in the bathroom. We took her to see our orthopedic surgeon in Phoenix, Dr. Howard Aidems. He too told us he had never seen anyone with five crushed vertebrae. He doubted she would ever walk again.

I can only say I decided that God did not want this for Linda and that somehow we would find someone to pray over her and she would be healed. I had been reading lots of books on healing by this time and there was allot of wonderful healing work going on in the church. In my mind, we just needed to find the right healer. Friends from Long Beach, California, Al and Barbara Regnier, whom we had met through Marriage Encounter called one day and told us that two Jesuit Priests, who also happened to be blood brothers, Dennis and Matthew Lynn, S.J., were going to be holding a workshop/retreat on healing in Orange County a few weeks later. We decided to go to the workshop. They said they would house us and go to the workshop with us.

In my mind I was sure someone associated with the workshop would see Linda on crutches and ask her what had happened. I was sure he/she would be touched by Linda's story, and that person would pass it along to one of the Lynn brothers who in turn would invite Linda on to the stage to be prayed over by them. I was sure that if the Lynn brothers were the ones to pray over Linda, her back would be healed. How is that for deciding how God should handle this situation?

We were having a wonderful spirit filled retreat. On Saturday afternoon Anita and I came back into the auditorium from a break only to see a woman associated with the retreat talking to Linda. I could tell from a distance that Linda was indeed telling the woman what had happened to her. About that time Father Matthew walked by and the woman reached out and pulled him over to meet Linda. My plan was unfolding right before my eyes. When the woman began to talk, Father Matthew started to fold his arm in what looked like a form of rejection. He found the right moment to interrupt the woman and then walked away. My plan seemed to be dead. It was clear to me by the facial expressions and other non-verbal motions that Linda would not be prayed over by the two priests who were giving the retreat.

Just before the dinner break, they announced that they would be addressing the subject of praying for physical healing after dinner. They then offered anyone needing prayers for inner healing to line up for some teams to pray over them. I did go for inner healing and experienced a very deep healing. I will talk more about this later.

After dinner, during their presentation, the Lynn brothers told us how they used to bring people who had a great need for physical healing up on stage. They would, in the past, lay hands on the person needing healing and healing usually occurred. They believed the overall effect was that people would believe, as I did coming to this retreat, that only "special people" had the gift of healing. They stated further that they believed most healing would occur when the persons who loved the recipient the most did the praying. In other words the best people to pray over Linda were Anita and me. Near the end of the talk they invited people to gather around those in need of prayer. Dennis Lynn led us in a very beautiful prayer for healing. We of course, along with our friends, laid our hands on Linda and prayed for her.

During the prayer Linda closed her eyes and in her imagination she saw herself lying on the ground. This incidentally had nothing to do with the words that were being prayed by Father Lynn. She then saw, in her imagination, Jesus walk by with a crowd following him. As Jesus got close she saw herself reach out and touch his clothes. As this happened in her imagination she said her head began to become very warm and slowly this warmth moved down her back to the area of the five crushed vertebrae. She said the constant pain she had been living with left her back. When the prayer ended we were all experiencing deep peace, and Linda had no more pain in her back. She, however, could still not stand without the crutches.

The Lynn brothers then introduced something they coined as "soaking prayer". They said their experience in the healing ministry lead them to believe that God often wanted people to soak their loved ones in prayer. They recommended a minimum of ten minutes a day and suggested we pray for however many days it took for any healing to be completed. They gave examples as to why this seemed to be desired by God in some situations.

We went home from the retreat determined to pray over

Linda for as many days as it took. The first evening at home when Anita and I went to pray over her, we realized we could not remember the beautiful words Father Dennis had used when he prayed during the retreat. I then thought what kind of a God would want us to pray the proper words, so I let go of my concern about that. We also realized ten minutes was a long time if you haven't practiced praying for that long. I can remember watching the clock as we prayed waiting for the ten minutes to go by. In some ways it was agony. We also did not know what words to use so we would fall back to praying Our Fathers and Hail Marys. On the third or fourth night of praying, Linda was lying on our bed in her robe. As we finished our ten minutes of praying we watched her five vertebrae decompress. Linda was still in a full cast for her broken leg, but she jumped up from the bed without her crutches, and with an angelic glow on her face she danced around the bedroom shouting "I've been healed! I've been healed!" Anita and I just sat there and cried tears of joy.

Chapter 4

Beginning of
Our Healing Ministry

I mentioned that Anita and I were coordinating a section of the southwest for World Wide Marriage Encounter. Fr. Mike had moved on to another position in the Encounter leadership by this time. Shortly after Linda's back was healed, the board we were heading up decided we should have a section wide convention; open to all encountered couples and priests. The board decided Las Vegas was a fairly central location that people could either drive or fly to if they wished. When the encounter would have such a convention, it was usually held at a Catholic school, rather than at a public facility, so the normal attraction of Las Vegas did not play into the equation. If people wanted to get into that sort of entertainment they would do so before or after the convention. I never heard of any people who did. These conventions started on Saturday morning, went all day Saturday and into Saturday evening, and usually ended with a closing Mass late Sunday morning, allowing people travel time to return to their homes in whatever city they came from. People were housed in the homes of the hosting community, so that was also part of the criteria of selecting a location. The format of these conventions was usually a series of talks given by a couple or a couple and a priest. Each talk was followed by reflection questions, time for the couples to talk about their reflections and often times small group sharing on the same subject.

Anita and I pushed for the inclusion of a talk dedicated

solely to the subject of forgiveness. This obviously came out of what we had been experiencing over the past year or so. We were selected to head up the outline committee. The other couples on the committee were all chosen from Arizona to cut down transportation costs and time.

We met one entire weekend and spelled out the outlines for all of the talks except the one on forgiveness. Time seemed to get away from us so the committee told us they would trust us to create the outline for that talk. We did decide, as a committee, that it would be given on Saturday evening after dinner.

A few weeks later Anita and I came to the conclusion that we had to step down from our leadership position because of my health. The new leaders who took our place asked us if we would be willing to give that particular talk at the convention despite the fact that we had resigned from our leadership responsibilities. We said we would be happy to do so.

It was a practice in the Marriage Encounter Movement to write your talks. There were a number of very valid reasons for this. Most of us were not accustomed to public speaking, the practice tended to keep the talks on focus, it prevented rambling, and it made it easier for two or three people (husband, wife, and priest presenting as a team) to interweave their talks etc.

Normally Anita and I always got our talks prepared well ahead of time. I will have to say Anita was always the driving force in this area. This time, however, we just did not get our talk prepared. The afternoon before we were supposed to leave for Las Vegas for the convention, Anita attended the closing Mass of a retreat that was being put on by Father Chuck Gallagher, S.J. for many of the priests of the Phoenix diocese. It seems that during the retreat some healing had taken place for the priests. One of the priests had told Father Chuck that he did not experience healing on the retreat and wanted some help with this before he returned to his parish. When Father Chuck saw Anita prior to the Mass he introduced her to the priest and told him that we, Anita and I, had the gift of healing. I don't know if this was being prophetic or not, but the priest insisted he see us that evening, so there went the last amount of time we had set aside to prepare our talk for the convention. The priest did not leave our house until close to midnight. The next evening we were driving to Las Vegas in a van that friends of ours were driving. We thought we would write the talks in the van, but we just did not get them done. To make a long story short, Saturday evening came and it was time to make our presentation. Just before we were introduced, Anita asked me in kind of a panicked voice what we were to do. I said "Lets pray." Anita prayed a simple prayer, "Come Holy Spirit..."

We walked up to the podium with a bunch of papers with a few notes written here and there. We talked from our hearts about what we had discovered about forgiveness in our recent journey with my nervous breakdown and Linda being attacked. When we finished we received a standing ovation from the two thousand or so people in attendance. People told us that night and on Sunday morning that they had experienced healing in their own lives as we talked. One couple told us that their daughter had been raped by five men some months earlier and that they had told no one. There were two priests from the Phoenix Diocese in attendance who asked us if we would give the same talk at their parishes. We did, and people who attended those talks had the same kind of experience, healing in their lives.

This experience led us, along with another couple and a priest, to put together outlines for a Friday night and all day Saturday retreat which would on healing. Since the five of us had come together through the Marriage Encounter experience we actually prayed that nobody with the Charismatic background would show up. I can only say we were very unsure of ourselves and we seemed to be threatened by people with a Charismatic background. We held our first retreat at a parish in Phoenix, and as near as I can tell, no one with that background showed up. At least no one in attendance held up their hands and shouted, "Praise the Lord."

Shortly after we had begun doing the retreats we had discontentment between the team members. Anita and I decided the turmoil was not worth it, and we decided to quit giving the retreats. We gave the outlines to the other couple and the priest and suggested they continue on their own. When people in the Marriage Encounter community heard that we had stopped giving the retreats, quite a few of them approached us and told us that we had the gift for healing and we should continue on our own. We thanked each of them and told them we would pray about it.

During prayers on this subject, we told God that we thought we could not do this ministry without a priest. The presence of a priest on the team opened doors at parishes that otherwise would not have been opened to us. In effect, we told the Lord that if He really wanted us to work in this ministry, He needed to send us a priest. The very next day Father Tom Owens, a priest of the Phoenix Diocese called and asked if he could stop over to talk to us about something. While he was at our house we asked him about joining us in the healing ministry. He said he would absolutely love to do it. We took that as a yes from God.

Chapter 5

The Beginning of My Healing

Before I go much further in this book, I think I would like to take the next couple of chapters to talk about some of the healings which took place in both me and in my daughter Linda, and in our entire family for that matter.

Earlier in the book, I allude to the fact that I had had what we refer to as a nervous breakdown. It was actually diagnosed as depression. In September of 1979 I had accepted a job to manage the software development for a product that the Intel Corporation was engaged in. I knew the vice president of engineering at this particular Intel department as he had been a VP of Engineering at Honeywell when I worked there as both a programmer and as a development manager. The job he hired me to do was to complete the development on a product that Intel was trying to get to market, but was not having much success. They were way behind schedule, and were facing stiff competition from other companies. I received a lucrative job offer with stock options so I took the job. The day I started working, the human resources representative walked into the conference room, filled with new employees, promptly at 8:00, flipped on an overhead projector, and said "Welcome to Intel. If you are not a workaholic, you probably will not last here."

During the weeks and months that followed we were under tremendous pressure to finish the development. I can honestly say I had never worked for such a well-run company. I can also say I had never worked in such a pressure cooker. In February of 1980 I told Anita one morning I just could not face going into work any longer. We realized my problem was really severe, so I decided to see a psychiatrist. After a visit or two to his office, he recommended I go into the Psychiatric Care Unit of Saint Joseph's hospital for treatment of depression. I came home from that visit and told Anita. Together we were stunned. We decided to call a friend, Father Murray Phalen. He suggested we drive over to his parish so we could talk. When we got there, we sat down in his office and he told us the idea of my needing to go into psychiatric care disturbed him greatly. He said right after he had hung up the telephone, he headed straight over to the church to pray before the Blessed Sacrament because he did not know what to tell us. The instant he said that he had gone before the Blessed Sacrament, I knew that somehow deep down I was going to be okay.

Father Murray suggested we get a second opinion. He even gave us the name of another psychiatrist. We made an appointment for the second opinion and after the consultation he also recommended hospitalization.

We were devastated, but into the hospital I went. We kept asking ourselves, "How could this be happening if we were doing God's work?" The first night in the hospital, they had some family counseling to help both Anita and me get used to the idea of my being in the psychiatric ward of the hospital. The person leading the session put up something like fifteen symptoms of depression on the white board. I could only relate to fourteen of them, so I told myself I must not be depressed. We call that denial, a subject I will discuss later, but in more depth. I was convinced the only real problem I had was the pressure from work. "If I just changed jobs all would be okay", I told myself. They also suggested we read a book called "The Angry Book." The next day I got permission to leave the hospital to run across the street to buy the book. I started to read it and could not put it down. I saw myself in almost every point the author was making. When I finished reading the book, I realized I was a very angry person who had managed to stuff my anger inside me, and that I was depressed, and the cause of the depression was this stuffed anger. I always thought that whenever I got angry it was the situation, something happening to me, that caused the times when I expressed anger.

During the week they also gave me a battery of tests. I remember two questions from the tests. One of those questions was, "do you love your father?" Without hesitation I answered "yes". The other question was, "do you love your mother?" I hesitated for some time, as I could not say yes, so I gave "no" as my answer. The discussions with my psychiatrist regarding the test results revealed I was very angry with my mother. The anger came from the fact that my mother would often get sick and she used her sickness to manipulate those around her to do what she wanted. There was a history of this for my entire life, and in fact my Aunt Elsie told me one time to do what she says, or she will get worse. She went on to say that my mother was that way even as a child. I also had a sense of guilt associated with my mother getting sick. One time when we were younger, we went to a Sunday school outing with my dad. While we were gone, my mother got sick and was taken to the hospital. When we got home, the lady that lived behind us laid a guilt trip on my dad saying he never should have taken us on the outing. Somehow as a sensitive child I apparently took on the guilt. That came out of the discussions with the psychiatrist.

In all fairness to my mother, I must say she was a wonderful person who worked very hard to keep the family going. For example, besides working full time in a job outside our home, mom baked two cakes virtually every day and then baked pretty much all day Saturday. My brother and I would eat one of the cakes before we went out to do the evening chores, and pretty much finished the other cake after dinner. We were big, fast growing teenagers who played sports in addition to doing the farm chores.

Now returning back to the hospital, because they kept a limited staff on the ward on weekends, we were allowed to go home for the weekend. Since Anita was teaching school, my father drove down to the hospital to bring me home on Friday afternoon. Dad shared the deep concern that he and mom had for me. When I told him how I had gotten in touch with a lot of anger, particularly with anger toward Mom, he indicated he understood. I went on to tell him that the doctor and staff had recommended I confront my mother with my anger as an effective way of dealing with it. I was not so sure about that, but at the same time I wanted to get well. When Dad was dropping me off at my house, he told me if confronting Mom would help me to get better, then that is what I should do. He said he wanted time to prepare her for what was to happen and that he would call me when they were ready for the confrontation. On Sunday morning, Dad called just before Anita and I, and the kids were leaving for Mass. He told me to come over after lunch, and that he had told Mom that I was also angry with him, so I needed to be prepared to share that anger as well.

At that moment I really was not in touch with any anger toward my dad, so at Mass that day I prayed that God would show me any anger I might have toward him and to give me the grace to say what needed to be said to both of them.

After lunch, Anita and I drove over to my parents' mobile home. I cannot even describe how tense I felt. In fact the whole room seemed to be filled with tension. I truly did not want to do what I was about to do, but I was desperate and I wanted to get rid of the depression I was in. When we got there we sat around their dining room table and talked very stunted small talk. You could cut the tension in all of us with a knife. Finally my father said, "Let's get this over with. Start with me." I closed my eyes and prayed and then began to speak. Much to the shock of all of us was the amount of anger that spewed forth from me directed at my father. I saw my father's jaw drop but he just let me dump all over him. When I was finished he asked for forgiveness and told me he loved me.

I then turned to my mother and the anger poured out of me like an erupting volcano. During my tirade my mother started to have an asthma attack as she had done so many times before in my lifetime. I screamed at her that I was not taking responsibility for her sickness any more. This one was on her! She immediately reverted back to normal breathing. After quite a few minutes of my dumping, my dad finally intervened and said enough had been said. My mother was in total shock and just sat there. Dad told me they loved me but it was time for me to leave so they could deal with all that had been said.

Anita and I left and went home. I was not sure whether it had been such a good idea to do what I had done. I told Anita I just needed to be alone to pray. Over the next few hours and in the days that followed I started to get a very deep sense of just how much my parents really did love me. Here they were in their seventies and they laid themselves out so that I could get better. I saw them, in effect, allowing themselves to be crucified so I could get well.

I spent two more weeks in the hospital, going home on the weekend in between. When I entered the hospital another Jesuit Priest Anita and I knew from Marriage Encounter called Anita and suggested to her that I repeat what was called an "aspiration" all throughout the day. In this particular aspiration he suggested I keep saying "Sacred Heart of Jesus, I put my trust in you." Not having been raised as a Catholic I had never heard of the Sacred Heart of Jesus before. For anyone reading this book who is in the same place one can think of it as the Heart of Jesus. Here too, I was willing to try anything that might help. While I knew that simply saying those words could be interpreted as superstition, I took it to mean simply putting my life in the hands (or heart) of Christ in the way I knew best. During the next two weeks I got more deeply in touch with hurts and anger in my life and began dealing with them. On the weekend off, we, Anita and I, traveled to Houston Texas to a Marriage Encounter leadership weekend. On Saturday night while sitting with a dozen or so couples and priests sharing our lives, someone asked what the meaning was of the bracelet I was wearing. When I told them it was a hospital patient identification bracelet, and that I was in the hospital being treated for depression, a flood of sharing opened up with several people there having some sort of healing because they had gone through a similar thing but had kept it very private. I shared about how many people had been praying for Anita and me and for our family and that the prayers were carrying us. In fact, it was on that weekend, I believe, when I found out that my close friend Al Regnier had been fasting for me for several weeks. It was incredible to be around a community of such deeply committed Christians.

The following week, my psychiatrist told me in all his years of practice he had never seen anyone get in touch with his feelings so quickly and so deeply. I told him it was the prayer and fasting that was lifting me up. I'm not sure he really understood what I was talking about, even though he was of the same faith. Unless someone had gotten involved in one of the renewal movements that were sweeping through the Catholic Church at that time they could not begin to understand it. It was what I believed Church should be like. In any case he told me he was releasing me from the hospital but he recommended I attend regular group therapy sessions conducted by one of his associates on an outpatient basis.

One thing I want to interject is that while lots of wonderful things were happening, I was still what I will call a basket case. I was far from being able to go back to work and live a reasonably productive life. It was an extremely difficult time for Anita, for me, and for our children. It was not very easy for anyone to be around me.

Chapter 6
Linda's Healing Process

People often ask how Linda is doing after the ordeal of having been attacked and injured and then having had her back healed. They almost always ask how she is doing emotionally. Most of the inquiries are out of genuine concern for her. Sometimes, however, there is almost a sense that there has to be something wrong, kind of like trying to show that God doesn't really heal, at least not totally. I don't know where this comes from, but I sense it is a mixture of unbelief and lack of knowledge with regard to God and healing. Mixed in at times, I am sure, is that someone I know and love didn't get healed so she must not really be healed. There is a plethora of teaching in the church with regards to God and healing. In fact there were many very powerful books written about the subject that came out of the Charismatic Renewal starting in the late 1960s. However, since healing is not a featured subject, if you will, in the everyday life of the church, many people have little or no knowledge with regard to the subject. This lack of knowledge about God's healing love and the general lack of belief in healing are all part, I believe, of that which contributes to this questioning.

I am hoping this book will draw people to seek what I believe God wants for us, particularly in the area of healing. It is an area that I talked about in the Introduction section of the book where we "place God in a box" defined by our limited knowledge and experience. It is a tough pill to swallow to see some get healed when someone whom I love does not experience healing.

One of the misconceptions people seem to get caught up in is that if the healing is not instantaneous, then God doesn't want me healed. We did not find this to be even close to the truth. Gradual healing over time was true for both Linda and for me. That is the healing did not take place all at once.

There are lots of factors in the healing process. Let me take a few minutes to tell you about the process Linda had gone through in the recovery (healing) from the despicable event that happened to her.

I told you in Chapter 3 about taking her to a retreat on healing, praying for her at the retreat, and then continuing to pray for her (soaking her in prayer) until her back was healed a few nights later.

Her second healing came through the medical profession. After being in a cast for some time for her broken leg, Dr. Aidem determined that the break would not set. One of the bones in the lower leg was broken, and the other bone had not broken. The solution was to have surgery and to saw the unbroken bone in half and reset both. We had many people praying and when the doctor came out of surgery the first words out of his mouth were that he had just experienced a miracle. He told us that the broken leg went back into place such that both legs would remain the same length. He had never seen that before. We thought that it was an interesting comment about having experienced a miracle coming from our doctor, who was of the Jewish faith.

Notice that in this case, her healing came through the hands of her doctor.

The next healing came when Linda got out of her cast after the operation. Her ankle had frozen in place and she had very little movement. The doctor sent her to physical therapy to try to free the movement in the ankle. When she came home for Easter break, I prayed over her ankle each evening while her mother was making dinner. She could feel and you could hear things breaking loose in the ankle as I prayed. Linda said it was similar to what was happening during physical therapy. After the second or third night she told me she did not want any more prayers and that she would stick with the physical therapy. By the strain in her voice I was compelled to question her about possibly still being upset with me for having taken the car away from her just before she was attacked. She said she had forgiven me, but did not want any more prayers. After some time in physical therapy, they told her they had done all they could, that she would always walk with a limp, and that she would never be able to wear high heels. She seemed to accept all of this.

Sometime afterward, when Linda was at home, we had a healing workshop at a local parish, and Linda decided to attend the workshop. On Saturday morning, we did a healing of memories in which we begin at conception and pray through time in the womb, in birth, early childhood, and right up through the adult years. The second part of the prayer is to have Jesus come to the person and communicate his love, and then to have Jesus bring in the people whom the person needs to forgive. Then we lead them through three levels of forgiveness. We call where this takes place the forgiveness room. In the afternoon, just before dinner, we have a foot washing experience taken from what the Linn brothers did in their workshop. In the foot washing experience, we encourage people to ask anyone with whom they need to reconcile, to wash their feet. If the person with whom they need to ask forgiveness is not present, then we encourage them to seek out someone to substitute for that person. During the foot washing Linda asked me to wash her feet. She told me that Jesus had brought me to her in the forgiveness room earlier that day, and that she wanted to ask for forgiveness for "holding onto anger" toward me for so long. I of course forgave her and washed her feet.

When the workshop ended that evening we all went home and went to bed. When Linda got up in the morning she stumbled a bit because her ankle had totally healed, and she had complete movement in her ankle restored.

Another healing took place during the semester at school after she had returned to the University of San Diego to resume classes. I had just finished reading about "healing the future" which I believe I read in one of the many books written by the Linn brothers. It turned out that Linda was developing a fear of going on each day and wanted to quit school and simply come home. Anita and I thought it might be better for her, in the long run, to find a way to work through this fear. So for several months we were on the phone with her every night listening to how she got through the day, building her up with praise and encouragement, and then praying her through each step of the way that she had to go through the next day. This whole process, we believe, was one of many things that kept her on the road to wholeness when it would have been easier to quit and become the victim, which in many ways she "earned the right" to be.

We have another healing. We mutually agreed that Linda should finish her schooling at the University of Arizona, where her two sisters were attending school. In that way, among other things, she would have the support of her sisters while at school. At the University of Arizona, they had a Friday holiday that had turned into a party weekend. At 3:00 A.M. Friday morning we got a call again. This time from her sister Cathy, telling us that Linda had been attacked again by a man, as she was leaving a party, and walking toward her car. We had Cathy put her in the car and drive her home. Anita and I went to morning Mass before they arrived at home. When we got back from Mass, both Linda and Cathy were in our bed asleep. While Anita made breakfast, and for an hour or so afterward, I prayed over Linda until she went into a deep restful sleep. When she awakened, we asked how she was doing, and her reply was something to this effect: she said she didn't know if this made any sense to us, but that she sensed that God was healing her while she slept, and that actually she felt very stable.

We also had her re-consult with Fr. Marc Calagary S.J. who had also helped counsel her through this whole ordeal whenever she was home. He worked quite a bit with her, helping her get in touch with the feelings she experienced in both attacks.

If we can move forward some twenty years, Linda is now married and has two children. On Halloween night after the youngest child was in bed and Linda's husband was out with the oldest child, Anita and I were getting ready to head home when Linda started complaining of pain in her lower back. The entire family was soon to head to San Francisco for the wedding of our second daughter, Lisa, which was to occur a few days later. Anita and I offered to pray over Linda and as we did, her back arched to the point where my hand and arm were pinned in a painful position. When I questioned her, she said she was not doing that. I began to pray in tongues and soon addressed a spirit of guilt. As soon as I addressed the spirit of guilt, Linda began to cry and state that the whole thing that happened to her twenty years earlier was her fault, as she should not have been walking home that evening when she was first attacked. We bound up the spirit, broke the power of the lies about her being the guilty party in the whole situation, and cast the spirit out of her. Within about five seconds all her back pain was gone.

A few years later, Anita and I attended another workshop given by the Linn's. In that workshop they brought home a concept about forgiveness that I had never heard before: that a person sometimes needs to have their feelings validated as part of the process of forgiving someone. Upon hearing this insight, I realized that never during this entire process had we done this for Linda. That is, we had not taken her feelings into account to the degree she needed. When we got home from the workshop, I called to ask for forgiveness. Her reply was that this was what Fr. Calagary had done with her, and that she believed we were not in the right condition to provide this for her at the time of the attack, as we had to deal with our own feelings as we all worked through the attack.

Linda currently teaches eighth grade religion at the local parish grade school, and she shares her story of God's healing love with her students. She has also gone back to school to get her teaching certification from the state. Because she is a part time teacher, she is not required to have the certification. In order to get certified she has had to take classes at night and go through student teaching, etc. Her husband is a successful business man so she really does not need to do this for the money it might provide. She told me she was praying about why she had an inner drive to get certified, when she realized she would have done all of this while still in college had it not been for the attack. She then realized this was the next step she was taking to get her life back from the grasp of her attacker.

Recently Linda informed us that she was training for a half triathlon, which is a race that includes a long swim, riding a bicycle for a long distance and then running for a long distance.

Yes, she is healed. Notice some of her healing was what some would call miraculous, and other parts of it came through the doctor, while others came through faith and determination. But in the end it is all from God.

Chapter 7

Who Needs Healing?

I want to take a few minutes to put healing in perspective. One of the questions that often surfaces is, "Do I need healing?" We found that most people deny any need for healing. There must be something wrong with me if I need healing is the thought process we seem to eventually get to. One of the questions I asked myself was, if no one needed healing then why did it seem to be a priority for Jesus when he walked this earth? It is easy to see from the scriptures that Jesus went about casting out demons (setting people free) and healing the sick. In Matthew 9 verses 12 and 13 it says:

> [12] He heard this and said, "Those who are well do not need a physician, but the sick do. [13] Go and learn the meaning of the words, "I desire mercy, not sacrifice. I did not come to call the righteous but sinners".

Jesus referred to himself as the physician and He was saying he came for people who needed his healing touch. One question which must be asked is, "Am I being self righteous when I deny any need for the healing touch of Jesus?" I think the answer is yes, indeed.

When Anita and I first started going through the process of healing we knew a group of married couples whom we met with regularly. When we brought the subject up to them every single person denied any need for healing. When we questioned them further we quickly discovered quite the opposite was true. Each and every one of them had wounds from their life experiences that were affecting how they lived and how they loved. What was even more interesting was once we got them to admit that they had these wounds, every one of them basically took on the attitude of "I'll just live with it." I talked to one friend about the fact that I thought he needed healing, and he told me very clearly he was not one of those people. He and his family lived in a very big house in a very fine neighborhood. He was a successful business man. He seemed to have that "Midas touch" in that with nearly every business undertaking, he was quite successful. Some fifteen or twenty years later, one day, he finally admitted that he had the need for healing.

So why do we need healing? At this point I am talking about what is called inner healing. I believe inner healing is closely related to physical healing, at least in some cases, but I'll get to that later.

The Gospel of Matthew (22:35-40) says the following:

> [35] Then one of them, a lawyer, asked *Him a question*, testing Him, and saying, [36] "Teacher, which is the great commandment in the law?" [37] Jesus said to him, *"You shall love the Lord your God with all your heart, with all your soul, and with all your mind."* [38] This is *the* first and great commandment. [39] And *the* second *is* like it: *"You shall love your neighbor as yourself.* [40] On these two commandments hang all the Law and the Prophets."

Jesus sums up the call for a Christian, that we love God and that we love others. Let's talk about this call.

What does it mean to love God? I used to think that to love God I had to go to church every Sunday, say my prayers, be good, be nice to people, and follow the Ten Commandments. In some ways I thought it was like missing all the fun, particularly the "being good" part. There were so many things the world had to offer that seemed like fun.

When I began to dig through the Scriptures I found the following in 1 John 5:3.

> [3] For this is the love of God, that we keep His commandments. And His commandments are not burdensome.

If we are only aware of the Ten Commandments, then loving God is like keeping the Ten Commandments. But Jesus tells us in the Gospel of John, chapter 15:

> [12] This is My Commandment, that you love one another as I have loved you.

We are to love one another. He also tells us to love our enemies in Matthew 5:43-48.

> [43] "You have heard that it was said, *'You shall love your neighbor* and hate your enemy.' [44] But I say to you, love your enemies, bless those who curse you, do good to those who hate you, and pray for those who spitefully use you and persecute you, [45] that you may be sons of your Father in heaven; for He makes His sun rise on the evil and on the good, and sends rain on the just and on the unjust. [46] For if you love those who love you, what reward have you? Do not even the tax collectors do the same? [47] And if you greet your brethren only, what do you do more *than others?* Do not even the tax collectors do so? [48] Therefore you shall be perfect, just as your Father in heaven is perfect."

It was the second part of 1 John 5:3 where He said that His commandments are not burdensome that kind of caught my eye. I slowly began to realize that the God I worship, the one who sent His only Son, Jesus, to die that I might be reconciled to the Father, really did love me and he wanted that which is best for me, and this included joy, peace, health and to be prospering in whatever I do. He is telling me the answer to all of this is in loving. Loving not only God, but loving others and loving self. Notice in Matthew 5 verse 45, above, he talks about becoming sons (and daughters) of God by loving. When one becomes a son or daughter, one receives from the Father as a son or daughter. We could write a book on this subject alone, but I hope you are beginning to see the picture. Loving is not an option if we are Christians. Also notice that God loves all of us, the just and the unjust. The vision I had of Jesus calling to Linda's attacker so he could heal him was certainly an example of that. The "perfection" in verse 48 of this Scripture is talking about the act of loving as God loves. In other words we are to love all people.

I also discovered Romans 8:28.

> [28] And we know that all things work together for good for those who love God, to those who are called according to *His* purpose.

This gave me hope. The answer to my struggles was nestled right in the scriptures and that I could focus on God's commandments to love and He would turn all things together to good. There are two things that really stand out to me in this passage. The first is that all things work *together* for good. It is the "things together" that is the point. All things that happen to us are not good in and of themselves. For example it is not good to lose one's job, but often times if we stay in faith, believing God's word, and then losing one's job just might be what had to happen to lead me to a better job. Also notice it says "all things work together for good for those who love God." I often hear people leave off the part about loving God and then wonder why things are not always working out so well.

During the period that I was working through my depression, I basically put my faith in this particular Scripture. I kept reminding myself that God would clean up the mess I was in as long as I put my focus on loving Him, which incidentally meant loving others and loving myself. For me, loving self is the hardest part, but we'll talk about that later.

Let's take a look at loving our neighbor. Before we go too far we need to have a definition of love. I think that love is a word in today's world that can mean almost anything. Rather than discuss all these definitions, let's go to the Scriptures.

In 1 Corinthians 4-8 Saint Paul gives us the definition of love for the Christian.

> [4] Love is patient, love is kind. It is not jealous, (love) is not pompous, it is not inflated, [5] it is not rude, it does not seek its own interests, it is not quick-tempered, it does not brood over injury, [6] it does not rejoice over wrongdoing but rejoices with the truth. [7] It bears all things, believes all things, hopes all things, endures all things. [8] Love never fails.

Go back and read that Scripture again, but this time read it slowly and carefully and while you are reading it, wherever it says love or where love is implied put your own name there. Ron is patient etc.

When I did this I became very uncomfortable. I saw all the times I lacked patience and all the times I became angry and on and on.

We have a plaque hanging on the wall by our kitchen table with this very scripture on it. It was one of Anita's favorite Scriptures. I personally did not like it as it made me uncomfortable. Then I started to ask questions about the Scripture. One of God's commandments is to love my neighbor. Love is defined as being patient and kind, etc. Earlier we talked about the love of God being defined as keeping His commandments. I actually asked myself if this were some sort of cruel joke. I saw the definition of love as not being attainable, at least not for me. No matter how hard I tried, I still lost my patience, I still was rude at times, and I often could not bear what was happening to me or around me.

However, when I began to go through inner healing for my depression I started to notice that I was becoming more patient, I could deal with what was happening to me and not blow up or fall apart, and I was doing this without even trying. I was beginning to have an inner peace I had never ever known before. I was beginning to experience some joy in my life; something that prior to the inner healing was also missing. Prior to experiencing God's inner healing, my joy tended to come from going to a party, drinking more alcohol than I should, and calling that joy. At least it seemed like joy, until the next morning when I woke up not feeling so well.

We discovered that inner healing is like weeding the garden and getting to the root of the problem, not just removing the tops of the weeds. Getting just the tops is like making behavior changes through will power. Making behavior changes through will power is good but I found that, sooner or later, the old behavior tended to pop up again, and just like a weed that has been lopped off, it eventually came back. Some of those times the behavior, when it came back, was worse than before, just like in a garden that has not been properly weeded. Inner healing gets to the root of the behavior and kills the weed so we can act like God calls us to act, that is, to love more deeply.

Allow Psalm 139:14-18 to touch you as you read it. Become aware of the parts of this wonderful Psalm that speaks to you,

> [14] I will praise You, for I am fearfully *and* wonderfully made; Marvelous are Your works, And *that* my soul knows very well. [15] My frame was not hidden from You, When I was made in secret, *and* skillfully wrought in the lowest parts of the earth. [16] Your eyes saw my substance, being yet unformed. And in Your book they all were written, The days fashioned for me, When *as yet there were* none of them. [17] How precious also are Your thoughts to me, O God! How great is the sum of them! [18] *If* I should count them, they would be more in number than the sand; When I awake, I am still with You.

I discovered that I needed to know that it was God who created me and that I am fearfully and wonderfully made. Knowing this has to be deep inside us, not just head knowledge. It has to be deep enough inside us that we just naturally live it out each and every day. We need to know that marvelous are His works, and that He thinks of each of us as precious. His thoughts for us out-number the grains of sand that exist. This message is the basis for love of self. Again we will talk more about love of self in greater detail. For now, just begin to love yourself more deeply than before.

Chapter 8
Does God Want Us Healed?

There is a question that often surfaces, that being, "Why isn't everyone healed?" Others ask it differently. They will say, "Why doesn't God heal everyone?" The question, when worded this way, seems to imply that God picks and chooses those whom he will heal. Those who are really deep into theology will tell us that God gives us illness for our good or to help in the process of redemption. I am just not that deep theologically. I prefer to approach the subject of God and His healing like a little child. I hurt, heal me Daddy. That is my approach to the subject.

I like the following scripture from Luke 11:9-13:

> [9] So I say to you, ask, and it will be given to you; seek, and you will find; knock, and it will be opened to you. [10] For everyone who asks, receives, and he who seeks finds, and to him who knocks it will be opened. [11] If a son asks for bread from any father among you, will he give him a stone? Or if *he asks* for a fish, will he give him a serpent instead of a fish? [12] Or if he asks for an egg, will he offer him a scorpion? [13] If you then, being evil, know how to give good gifts to your children, how much more will *your* heavenly Father give the Holy Spirit to those who ask Him!

We can talk about this Scripture for a long time, but for now I just want to focus on one aspect. What father of mother would not want to heal his or her own child? Jesus tells us in this scripture that God the Father will give more than any of us as sinners can give. He gives us the

Holy Spirit if we ask Him, and it is by the power of the Holy Spirit that healing takes place. If you want to delve into this subject, the Power of the Holy Spirit and why we don't see a lot of healing in many of our churches, get the book "The Nearly Perfect Crime," written by Francis Mac Nutt. He has some interesting points on the subject. You can "GOOGLE" Francis Mac Nutt on the internet, go to his website and order the book.

A friend of mine, who is a medical doctor asked me the question about why doesn't God heal everyone. I turned the question back to him with a series of questions. I asked him, "As a physician do you pick and choose whom you are going to heal?" "Of course not", he answered. "So you would agree that a doctor pretty much always wants to heal the patient (excluding fraudulent doctors and quacks)," I said. He agreed. "So, do all your patients get healed?" "No, not all patients get healed," was his answer. "So if you have two patients with the same problem and all the other factors are pretty much the same, height, weight, age etc., and if you prescribe the same dosage of medicine to both, then it must be the medicine, right?" was my next question. By this time he was getting exasperated with me but his answer was very clinical, at least for this lay person. He said he believed the medicine is sufficiently controlled and tested to be the same dosage for both. "What are you getting at, Ron Heyn?" he asked. My answer was simple, "If you, as a physician don't pick and choose whom you are going to heal, and if the medicine is the same for both parties, then the condition of the person not getting healed probably has more to do with the patient than the doctor." At least that is the way I approached my own healing. I have since learned that it has more to do with the person praying than it does with the person being prayed for. In the 16th chapter of Mark it says:

[15] And he said to them, "Go into all the world and preach the gospel to the whole creation. [16] He who believes and is baptized will be saved; but he who does not believe will be condemned. [17] And these signs will accompany those who believe: in my name they will cast out demons; they will speak in new tongues; [18] they will pick up serpents, and if they drink any deadly thing, it will not hurt them; they will lay their hands on the sick, and they will recover."

In verse 17 Jesus says "these signs will follow those who believe" and in the 18th verse he says "they will lay hands on the sick and they will recover."

I was not aware of what was told to us by Jesus, at least I did not catch the point about when we believe these things will happen. So I told myself that if I was not getting healed, then I must be blocking God's healing grace. In fact, during the time I was coming out of the depression, much of my prayer was to ask God what was it in me that was blocking my getting healed, and then I would listen for the answer. We'll talk more about that process later in the book. Let's get back to what can possibly be a block to healing. At least what appears to be a possible block to being able to experience inner healing.

At the highest level I discovered two major blocks to healing. One is pride (self-righteousness) and the other is fear. I think it is interesting that both of these are what I will call enemies of faith (believing). I am sure there are more, but we'll talk about these two for now. In another chapter we'll talk about what role "giving and asking for forgiveness" can play in this as well.

One aspect of pride and perhaps fear, depending upon how you look at the next Scripture is that we must face the question, Do I want to be healed? Let's look at John 5:1-14.

[2] Now there is in Jerusalem by the Sheep *Gate* a pool, which is called in Hebrew, Bethesda, having five porches. [3] In these lay a great multitude of sick people, blind, lame, paralyzed, waiting for the moving of the water. [4] For an angel went down at a certain time into the pool and stirred up the water; then whoever stepped in first, after the stirring of the water, was made well of whatever disease he had. [5] Now a certain man was there who had an infirmity thirty-eight years. [6] When Jesus saw him lying there, and knew that he already had been *in that condition* a long time, He said to him, *"Do you want to be made well?"* [7] The sick man answered Him, "Sir, I have no man to put me into the pool when the water is stirred up; but while I am coming, another steps down before me." [8] Jesus said to him, *"Rise, take up your bed and walk."* [9] And immediately the man was made well, took up his bed, and walked. And that day was the Sabbath. [10] The Jews therefore said to him who was cured, "It is the Sabbath; it is not lawful for you to carry *your* bed." [11] He answered them, "He who made me well said to me, 'Take up your bed and walk.'" [12] Then they asked him, "Who is the Man who said to you, 'Take up your bed and walk?'" [13] But the one who was healed did not know who it was, for Jesus had withdrawn, a multitude being in *that* place. [14] Afterward Jesus found him in the temple, and said to him, *"See, you have been made well. Sin no more, lest a worse thing come upon you."*

I see two major points, and perhaps a third that I will talk about. As with most scriptures we can dissect it into lots of discussions, but for now let's stick to the three points.

The first is the question that Jesus asked, "Do you want to be made well?" A knee jerk reaction would be, "Of course I want to be healed. Who wouldn't want to be healed?" If you noticed the man never answered the question, he talked all about his misfortune, about not getting to the water quickly enough.

When I was in the hospital, once I became accustomed to it, the thought of having to go back into the real world was very scary for me. I could not handle any kind of stress and my hospital stay was relatively free of stress. The only responsibilities I had to deal with were to make my bed each day and to attend the various sessions they set up for me such as group therapy. For that I had three meals a day, a roof over my head and essentially no stress. During my hospital stay I actually looked up the laws regarding insurance and social security to see if I could reasonably care for my family and never have to leave the hospital. I quickly realized I could not do that for financial reasons. So it was the love for Anita and my children combined with the reality that there was no sugar daddy insurance program that would keep me there very long. I had to face my fears and get well, well enough to function in society such that I supported my family. Otherwise I would likely still be in the hospital.

One time I was asked to give a teaching to the local men's prayer group here in Phoenix. I don't remember how we decided on the subject but it was decided I would give the teaching on "the role of the community in healing." By the community, I mean whatever community you are part of. For example, my family is one of the communities I am part of. I was at Mass one Sunday morning and had been praying for some insight as to what to include in the teaching. What God revealed to me was that up to that point in my life I had never, in my entire life, gone to see a doctor without either my mother (when I was younger) or my wife, Anita, (after I was married) telling me that "I needed to go to the doctor." I believe the reluctance on my part as a man, to admit I needed a doctor for healing, was pride.

I cannot even begin to tell you about the number of people who basically tell me they don't need healing. Or, they say something like I will get through this on my own. I think this can be categorized in the pride column.

I want to add one more thing regarding fear and its role in the healing process. I found it to be very fearful to face some of the feelings I had deep inside me and the only way I could do it was to believe that God is my healer and that I had to walk through those fears no matter how strong the fear was. I just clung to the fact that God would get me through anything and everything I had to face. In an example I talk about in Chapter 14 of this book I don't think I would have persevered because of the fear I was experiencing as I was prayed for, had I not clung to the fact that God was moving in this and He would make it all work.

Chapter 9

Let's Talk About Forgiveness

Let's talk about forgiveness. First, the act of forgiving others and, later we will talk about the act of asking for forgiveness. When I got out of the hospital I started to read books about God's healing. In fact, I can remember a Saturday evening when I was reading a book called Healing Prayer, authored by Barbara Shlemon, a lay person in the Catholic Church who was deeply involved in the healing ministry. I believe the book has been revised and the author is now Barbara Shlemon Ryan. In any case I jumped up and ran into the other room to tell Anita that God was still healing people and it was through God where I needed to look for my healing. Anita got very nervous and questioned me if I was going to stop my psychiatric care. I assured her I wasn't but that I had a new hope that somewhere somehow God was going to heal me. I continued to read books on the subject of God's healing love and I began to see a thread that spoke out to me. That thread was forgiveness, particularly the act of forgiving others throughout my entire life.

It helps me to understand forgiveness and its effect on me by breaking it down into categories. So let's do that. We'll begin with why we must forgive if we want to experience all the grace God has for us.

When Jesus hung on the cross he said "Father, forgive them, they know not what they do." (Luke :23:34). As Christians, followers of Christ we are called to put on the mind of Christ. We are called to forgive. Let's look at some additional scriptures.

In the 6ᵗʰ chapter of Matthew, Jesus was teaching his disciples and when he came to prayer He gave them the prayer that we call the "Our Father" or the "Lord's Prayer". Notice that in the prayer it asks God to forgive us in the same way we forgive others.

(Matthew 6) ⁹ This is how you are to pray:

"Our Father in heaven,
hallowed be your name,
¹⁰ your kingdom come,
your will be done,
on earth as in heaven.
¹¹ Give us today our daily bread;
¹²and forgive us our debts,
as we forgive our debtors;
¹³ and do not subject us to the final test,
but deliver us from the evil one."

After giving His disciples this way to pray Jesus went on to say the following:

(Matthew 6) ¹⁴ "If you forgive others their transgressions, your heavenly Father will forgive you. ¹⁵ But if you do not forgive others, neither will your Father forgive your transgressions."

If you read that literally, it tells us that God won't forgive us unless we forgive others. I personally have trouble with that in light of God's total and complete love for us. I prefer to think of it as Jesus telling us that if we do not forgive others we are made such that we cannot receive God's forgiveness. The result on us is the same whichever way we look at the passage, that is, by not forgiving others we cannot or do not experience the grace of God's forgiveness of us.

I like to think of it as shutting down a faucet. Scripture

talks about the living waters of the Holy Spirit and how His love flows through us. Well I like to think of "not forgiving" as being analogous to shutting down or shutting off the flow of God's love in us.

So what does this have to do with healing? I have heard teachings say that our forgiving others has nothing to do with healing. That God can heal us anyway. And that is true. There are lots of instances in the word of God where Jesus heals a person and forgiveness does not seem to come into play. However, if I were going to err on this subject I would err on the side of forgiving those who hurt me. Read on.

In the Gospel of Matthew in chapter 18 verses 21 through 35 there is a long discussion of forgiveness. Let's look at it.

> [21] Then Peter approaching asked him, "Lord, if my brother sins against me, how often must I forgive him? As many as seven times?" [22] Jesus answered, "I say to you, not seven times but seventy times seven times."

The first part deals with how many times must we forgive. Peter asks Jesus if we can put a limit on this, by asking must we forgive as many as seven times, which I would take to mean that seven times is my limit. But Jesus says, you don't put a limit on how many times we must forgive. Anita and I have been married over 50 years and we hurt each other often. If we put a limit on how many times we had to forgive each other before we throw in the towel, we would not be married any longer.

I like to insert in a little joke about these two passages to make a point. We are told that we can only live in the now. So if we limit this passage to just today, and if we sleep eight hours a day, and if we take the passage literally, seventy times seven times is 490 times. If we divide 16 hours (which is 960 minutes) by 490 we need to forgive about every 1.9 minutes. The point is we have to forgive often and without limit.

Jesus went on with His teaching about forgiveness with the following parable:

> [23] That is why the kingdom of heaven may be likened to a king who decided to settle accounts with his servants. [24] When he began the accounting, a debtor was brought before him who owed him a huge amount. [25] Since he had no way of paying it back, his master ordered him to be sold, along with his wife, his children, and all his property, in payment of the debt. [26] At that, the servant fell down, did him homage, and said, "Be patient with me, and I will pay you back in full." [27] Moved with compassion the master of that servant let him go and forgave him the loan. [28] When that servant had left, he found one of his fellow servants who owed him a much smaller amount. He seized him and started to choke him, demanding, "Pay back what you owe." [29] Falling to his knees, his fellow servant begged him, "Be patient with me, and I will pay you back." [30] But he refused. Instead, he had him put in prison until he paid back the debt. [31] Now when his fellow servants saw what had happened, they were deeply disturbed, and went to their master and reported the whole affair. [32] His master summoned him and said to him, "You wicked servant! I forgave you your entire debt because you begged me to. [33] Should you not have had pity on your fellow servant, as I had pity on you?" [34] Then in anger his master handed him over to the torturers until he should pay back the

whole debt. [35] So will my heavenly Father do to you, unless each of you forgives his brother from his heart?

When Jesus died on the cross He forgave us our entire debt. He wiped it clean and we are to do the same with little debts.

There are four points, and perhaps more, that Jesus makes in this parable. One is that we are to forgive the little debts (little compared to what we have been forgiven for). Most of us don't have big hurts, but we do have lots of little hurts. A husband and wife easily hurt each other with things like cutting remarks or anger when things don't go as planned. There are often lots of put downs not only in a marriage, but we put our children down when their grades are not up to our expectations or when they fail to clean their rooms. The list goes on and on. In family relationships the little hurts include a failure to thank our spouse for whatever they have done for the family, like going to work every day, for cooking and cleaning, etc. After a while these little hurts build up into bigger wounds.

What we discovered was that when not dealt with these little hurts build into mountains and pretty soon the relationship is broken.

A second point is that we are to forgive because we have been forgiven. God has forgiven us much and he has forgiven us totally and we are to do the same. This is stated clearly in Colossians chapter 3, verse 12.

> [12] Put on then, as God's chosen ones, holy and beloved, compassion, kindness, lowliness, meekness, and patience, [13] forbearing one another and, if one has a complaint against another,

forgiving each other; as the Lord has forgiven you, so you also must forgive.

The third point is that the master had the person who did not forgive the small debt turned over to the torturers. I am told by a scripture scholar that this is one of Jesus' references to hell. This is what we often see in family relationships; husband and wife, children and parents, or siblings with each other. When the little hurts go unattended, life in the family starts to become a little hell hole. Many who are reading this will deny that this is the case in their family, but then why are there so many divorces and so many teenage suicides? Or why are so many people turning to drug and alcohol to get through life? As the love relationship starts to break down we slowly start to live in the torturous state of isolation, loneliness, and lack of communication. The list goes on. Most family messes don't come from one incident, but rather an accumulation of lots of little wounds that slowly tear us apart.

The fourth point that Jesus makes is that this will happen to us unless we forgive each other from the heart and not just with the head. This was the point, forgiving from the heart, which jumped out at me when I was going through my recovery (healing).

When I was in the hospital the doctor told me I had a lot of anger, and he was correct. What he suggested I do was to go around and tell those who had hurt me how angry I was. Blow off the steam, and if possible, do it with those who had hurt me. That is what I did the first weekend after being in the hospital, with my mother and my dad. I will have to say that it did create some form of relief, but it did not heal me. When I approached my psychiatrist with the subject of forgiving those who hurt me, he responded in such a way that made me begin to rethink the entire process. He told me in no uncertain terms that in his professional opinion the "forgiveness was a bunch of B.S", only he spelled out B.S. I was really shocked by this in that I was being treated in a Catholic Hospital by a doctor who claimed to be of the Catholic faith, and who had actually studied to be a priest. In all fairness to him, after reading the passage quoted above, especially the part about forgiving from the heart I came to the conclusion that most of my experience of forgiveness appeared to be B.S. The reason was that I had to admit I had never really forgiven from the heart. When Anita and I began to talk about it we agreed it was true for both of us, that is, in a lot of instances we had never really forgiven from the heart.

We could easily see many areas where we had not forgiven from the heart. One of the telltale signs was that we would score keep. When a little hurt occurred more than once, we would often respond with something like, "This is the 10th time this week that you have done that." Another sign of not having forgiven from the heart is avoiding situations in our relationship where we had been hurt before.

What we started to discover was that lack of forgiveness, or forgiveness which was not from the heart, put a wedge in our relationship. We looked back at our family experiences growing up and could easily remember broader family wedges. Certain relatives would not come over for Christmas or a birthday because an argument had occurred and one or more parties were not talking to each other.

We see many people who have left the church because someone in the church offended them by what was said or how it was said. My own father only went to church on Easter and Christmas Eve, at best, because he said a minister had given him a dirty look when he only put a nickel in the collection plate. My opinion of that was that maybe he was feeling a sense of guilt for only putting a nickel in the collect plate. If that were true then he needed to forgive himself, not refuse to go to church and blame someone else for his feelings. This incident had occurred years before I was born and he still harbored the anger. I could go on forever with examples both inside my own family and outside as well, but hopefully you have gotten the point.

You may be asking at this point what does this have to do with healing? Let me say this. There have been lots of studies that show tendencies in people to become ill, based on how much anger they carry around. I know this from my own experience how much energy it took for me to keep my anger stuffed all those years. Luckily it showed up in me as depression and not some fatal sickness.

A person who is carrying around un-forgiveness is not at ease. We can reword that and say he is in disease.

Before I go on to the next chapter I must say that as a Christian I must forgive because God forgave me. Jesus says we are to follow Him. To follow Jesus means we are to live our lives as He lived His. He has given us the model for life as a Christian. This means forgiving is not optional.

Chapter 10
Signs of Hurting People

We talked a little bit about what happens when we don't forgive. But let's expand that subject particularly in light of our call to love one another. It is often easier to see the point being made when talking about the husband and wife relationship and in the family relationship. Keep in mind this is true in all relationships. In fact, if I come home from work angry at the driver who cut me off, or who slowed me down in traffic, I carry that into the family relationship unless I have dealt with it.

What we discovered in our ministry is that there are a number of sin patterns that wounded people (those in need of inner healing) live out. I am going to talk about these patterns to help you, the reader, if perhaps you have a need to deal with un-forgiven hurts. I call them sin patterns because these behavior patterns break down one's relationship with other people, the same people God calls His followers to love.

Let's talk about five sin patterns that a hurting person falls into. I am sure there are more than five, but these five will catch many of the cases. The five patterns are anger, apathy, irresponsibility, criticism and pride (including independence). We'll talk about each in turn.

When we look anger we are not talking about getting angry, as that can be a healthy response to a situation. I mean if someone steals from me or whacks me on the side of the head, an angry response is quite normal and is healthy. Denying the anger can lead to problems later (stuffed anger). Holding onto the anger is also not healthy. What we are talking about here is the person who is generally angry. I fell into this category, only I never recognized it because I always thought the anger was caused by someone or something else. I also stuffed a lot of anger because I was Christian and I thought it was wrong to be angry. The problem was that the anger would come out later and it would be much stronger. When I went into the hospital and was diagnosed with depression, the staff recommended a book called The Angry Book, written by Theodore Isaac Rubin, M.D. I got permission to leave the hospital for a few minutes to run across the street to a book store where I bought the book. When I started to read it, I could not put it down. I am a slow reader, but I finished the book in one day. I related to so many examples in the book that I think it was a jump start to my recovery process. The fact that I could admit that I had anger issues went a long way to getting to some of the base issues of the depression I was living with.

A lot of people don't think they carry any anger. Some are just annoyed easily. That is anger. Others think the anger comes from a stimulus outside of oneself, like I did. One way to honestly test this is to see how others react to the same stimulus. If I am reacting strongly to something and those around me are not, then I need to look inside myself. Other people who carry a lot of anger simply avoid situations that stimulate the anger in them. After a while these people are trapped in their own small world, driven by avoiding situations that trigger the anger inside them.

That leads us into the second sin pattern which I mentioned earlier, called apathy. People who are hurting sooner or later tend to withdraw from relationships. They give up on life. Jesus said we are to love one another. Some people think the opposite of love is anger. It is not. The opposite of love is apathy, withdrawing from relationship. The church is full of apathetic people. These are the uninvolved, don't care kind of people. We see that in many marriages. Two people living under the same roof basically uninvolved with one another. They just don't seem to have the desire or the energy to be involved. Jesus said you will know my disciples by the way they love one another. He also said "A new commandment I give to you. Love one another". Love is not a feeling it is an action word, a decision to be involved with the other. When Anita and I have hurt one another we often withdraw one from the other. And this is okay if we are withdrawing to gather ourselves, perhaps to pray to work through and forgive the hurt. But withdrawal as a coping mechanism is apathy. We each live out this apathy in different ways. I tend to turn inward and simply smolder inside. Anita says she makes herself busy with a project or she starts cleaning the house. So I like to joke and say if I come home and find the house really clean, then we just might have a problem we need to address.

The third sin pattern is irresponsibility. When we are hurting we often turn to irresponsible behaviors, such as over eating, drinking excessively, drugs, or even shopping. Yes this can be an irresponsible behavior. The world around us tells us that if you are feeling bad, go buy something. I am not saying it is wrong to shop, but if the reason we are shopping is to kill the pain, then we need to take another look at our behavior. If this is not a sinful pattern then why are so many people maxed out on their credit cards. Besides, buying something is only a temporary fix. We may feel good having bought something we don't need, but it doesn't take long before we are feeling the pain again. Two of the pain killers I like to turn to are eating and/or alcohol when I don't like what I am feeling. Others are workaholics, drug addicts (or casual users). The list goes on. These are all sinful patterns because they stress the family, they stress the family income, and they cause us to run from the love relationships we are called to have.

The fourth sinful pattern is criticism, the act of putting another person down. Criticism has no place in a love relationship. In fact I believe criticism has no place in the heart of a Christian. Criticism kills a relationship. It is not life giving in any form. Some people say they use constructive criticism. There is nothing constructive about criticism. Criticism is destructive. Some people confuse criticism with correction. It is okay and even life giving to correct someone. Criticism includes name calling. When we criticize, we are putting down one of God's creations. Wow, to think we can judge one of His creations and show what is wrong with it! Let's take a simple example of the difference between a criticism and a correction. Let's say a child's room is a mess. A criticism would be to call the child a slob with the way he/she keeps his/her room. A correction would be to say the room must be cleaned up before you can go out, or whatever. A number of years ago, when we were involved in leadership in the Marriage Encounter movement, and all of our children were still living at home, we decided as a family, to create a criticism can. We agreed that Anita and I would put 25 cents in the can every time we criticized anything. The children agreed they would put 5 cents in the can when they criticized. We all agreed the fine would be double if we criticized in prayer. In prayer you ask? Yes, since I was a master in sarcasm, a form of criticism, it would not be unusual for me to sarcastically add a thank you to God when one of the kids cleaned their room or did some other chore they were expected to do. So it is not just what we say, but the tone of voice we use. One time I made a comment as Mass was ending about how dead the parish seemed to be. The children said that would be double. I argued that I was not praying, but they all retorted that it was in the house of prayer. In went 50 cents. So, in a sense we had some fun with the idea. Well, we did this during Lent and gave the money to the poor box when Easter came. Our family ended up putting in over $50.00 during those six weeks with the majority of it coming in the first few weeks. The kids even remarked that they became so aware of criticism that they had come to realize they had friends and classmates who basically lived on criticism. The opposite of criticism is praise. We began to praise each other, which led to praising others as well. It really had a profound effect on our family. The more we praised the children, the more they lived up to the praise. We told them things like how proud we were of how hard they studied, even though their grades did not always reflect it. Before long they were studying harder and their grades went up. One day I called Anita sexy and she responded with a big smile. I thought, "Wow". So I started to tell her how sexy she was every day. In fact every time we were apart and came back together. I can only say "Wow!" Anita's mother was, I am sorry to say, very critical of Anita. I know she wanted the best for Anita, but being critical did not help her in any way. We had reached the point in our lives when Anita's mother was coming over for dinner every evening. When we would sit down to eat she seemed to find fault with whatever Anita served. She even criticized things like the fruit she had bought at the market. I was praying one day and I got this bright idea. Before her mother could criticize anything at the meal, I would tell Anita this was the best meat loaf she had ever made. Or I would say I loved the way she cooked the string beans. When she served fruit at the end of the dinner I would tell her how great the oranges were that she had gotten at the market. Let me interject for a moment that Anita was a very busy person as she taught Spanish full time, handled the four kids, and had her mother over for dinner each night. I was working long hours as a computer programmer. One of the things my wife's family often did was reheat leftover Italian bread in the oven when preparing dinner. Anita carried this practice into our marriage, which I, being a big eater, loved. As she got more and more pressured over time, Anita started to have a tendency to put the bread in the oven and forget that it was there. I loved the smell of the bread warming up but would get very annoyed, if not upset, when the bread came out of the oven burned. During this period, it seemed like this was happening more and more often. A couple of things happened as a result of my praising her cooking each night. First her mother looked at me like I had three heads when I would pour out the praises on Anita's cooking. It did accomplish what I had hoped, and that is, she stopped criticizing Anita's cooking. After a couple of months of praising her cooking, I was praying one day when I became overwhelmed as to how blessed I was to have Anita as my wife. It was like my heart had changed dramatically and I didn't even realize it needed changing. The third thing that happened was Anita stopped burning the bread.

The fifth sin pattern is pride. When we are filled with pride we do not let anyone get close to us. We see ourselves as so capable that we don't need anyone else. It is almost impossible to have a love relationship with a prideful person. One of the more devastating attributes of pride is privacy. By that I mean I don't want anyone to see I need help, that I need prayers. I cannot imagine what state I might be in if we had not called for prayers when I realized I needed to go into the hospital (or Looney bin, as I lovingly referred to it) to find out what was wrong with me. We had so many people praying that the doctor handling my case told me he never had a patient get in touch with his feelings as fast as I did. People were not only praying but they were also fasting for me. Then when Linda got attacked we put out the call for prayers immediately. We watched miracles happen. Some people thought it was terribly wrong for us to make public what had happened to her. My answer to that is, how do you get the body of Christ to help absorb the pain unless you engage the body in prayer?

Chapter 11
Whom We Need To Forgive

The question of whom to forgive needs to be answered. In general terms there are three people we need to forgive. Obviously we need to forgive others. By others I mean the people in our lives that have hurt us in some way or another. It does not matter whether or not the hurt was intentional. But there are two others we need to forgive. Sometimes we need to forgive God. Yes, we need to forgive God. You will be surprised how many people lay the blame for things on God. The third person we need to forgive is ourselves. We will talk about each person in turn.

Let's start with forgiving others. It was through prayer experiences such as the healing of memories that I not only discovered whom I needed to forgive but also how to forgive them. One can start by simply asking Jesus to show us whom we need to forgive. I do this in a number of ways but basically I ask Jesus whom I need to forgive and then I sit quietly in prayer until He brings people to my mind. When I realize I need to forgive someone, I pray a simple prayer that goes something like this: I pray from my heart to forgive the person. I then ask God to bless the person just as they are. Finally I ask Jesus to forgive that person through my heart. For some of the hurts and/or some of the people I find I have to do this every day, sometimes for days or weeks. I know I prayed for the man who attacked Linda for at least eight or ten years. The same was true for forgiving my mother. I am not sure if I needed to pray for forgiveness for all that time. All I know is that I felt no form of love toward her for many years after my nervous breakdown. Let me explain. I was not consciously aware of this at the time but sometime after my mother died, my dad told me that when I was born my mother was too sick to care for me. In addition to this my mother never seemed to be able to express any form of physical affection. I seldom remember her hugging me, and when she did, she was stiff and cold as a fish. I asked my dad who took care of me those first years of my life. He told me that my aunt Elsie, my mother's younger sister, came to the house every day and cared for me. When he told me this I realized I had spent my entire life thinking there was something wrong with me that I loved my aunt Elsie, but could not warm up to or have feeling for my mother. I had never told anyone this. In fact it never came up when I was in the hospital receiving psychiatric care. With this background I prayed to forgive my mother for her lack of motherly love as well as the many ways she seemed to use her illness to manipulate the family to try to kill her own pain.

I need to take a minute to tell you how God worked through all the praying I did to try to reconcile myself with my mother. One day during this long multi-year period of praying every day to forgive my mother, she became ill (which she often did throughout my life) and was hospitalized. By the way, we had come to expect this almost every year. My mother would get sick, be hospitalized for a couple of weeks and then would get well. When she returned home, all she seemed to talk about was how much attention she had received from the doctors and the staff at the hospital. Lucky for my dad, she worked at the hospital not too far from our farm, so the cost was minimal or free.

In any case, this particular time she was so sick that my brother decided to fly out to Phoenix from upstate New

York to say his goodbyes to her, as it looked like she was not going to make it. One day while he was here, I was at work and I took a few moments to pray. While praying I got the sense that God was telling me to go home to my dad's house where my brother was staying. My boss, who was a good Christian man said, "Go take whatever time you need." When I got there my brother told me that my mother's lungs had filled with fluid and after they had gone into her lungs to pull the fluid out, the lungs had filled again within a couple of hours. When they wanted to go into her lungs again, she had refused, saying it was too painful. We talked about it and my dad said her wish was for no extraordinary procedures to keep her alive. I asked dad if she knew she was dying. He said he did not know if she knew that or not. I asked if it would not be proper to tell her that she was going to die without this procedure and then let her make the decision. We all agreed that she should know that. We also agreed that dad was far too upset to tell her and that my brother and I should be the ones to tell her. Consequently, the two of us left for the hospital immediately.

On the drive over, my brother who is older than me, said that I was better at this kind of thing than he was, and that I should do the talking. I have to say that if I was not sure the Holy Spirit was involved in all of what was happening, I would have objected on the grounds that as the older son he should do the talking. Who wants to tell his mother she is going to die?

When we got to the hospital she was in Intensive Care. She could barely speak. After a few minutes of the two of us holding her hands from either side of the bed I broached the subject. I told her I understood she had denied the doctors from going back into her lungs to remove the fluids. She nodded this was true, and whispered it just hurt too much and that she wanted antibiotics to kill the infection. I gently told her she was on triple doses of antibiotics and they were not working. I asked her if she understood what I just told her. She nodded that she understood. I asked her if she knew what that meant with regards to her condition. She indicated she did not really know what it meant. I then, as gently and as lovingly as I could, told her she would probably die. I also told her if she wanted to go home to be with the Lord that we would let her go. She just lay there with her eyes closed and asked where the children were, that she wanted to see them. The previous Sunday after Mass, a nun at our parish, knowing my mother was in serious condition, had given me a very quick course on death and dying. When mom asked to see the children that seemed to tell me she was getting ready to go home to the Lord. Two of our children were away at college so I asked her if she could hang in there until Friday evening, if she needed to. She looked up and whispered that Friday would be fine, that she was much stronger than they thought. What my mom did not know was that her condition was such that she would most likely suffocate from not being able to process the oxygen because of the fluid in her lungs. After a long pause, my mother looked up and squeezed both of our hands and told me that in all of her entire life, nobody had ever talked to her with such tenderness, and that she had never experienced such love in her life. She said she wanted to go on living and that the doctor could take the fluid from her lungs. I am not sure about the depth of what my brother experienced but we were all crying. What I can tell you was that for the first time in my life, I experienced a deep sense of love for my mother.

We left the hospital and told dad what had happened and that he needed to call the doctor's office to have the doctor schedule the procedure to remove the liquid from her lungs again. I then headed back to my office to continue working. Two or three hours later, my brother called to tell me the hospital had called to say that my mother's lungs had completely cleared up without medical attention. The doctor came in, examined her and released her from Intensive Care. The next day she came home from the hospital and lived for another three or four years. My God is amazing.

I am going to save forgiveness of self for last. Why? I have found this to be the most difficult of the three. Let's take a few moments and talk about forgiving God. I have come to believe the biggest reason we blame God for things that happen in our life is that we have never been truly taught just how much God loves us. In the main line churches we have basically been taught that we have to earn God's love (by not sinning). This being said, when we have a twisted view about God and His love for us, I think it is quite natural for a person to be angry with God when they lose a loved one, and especially, but not limited to, losing a child. First, it is out of the natural order for a child to die before one's parents. This alone makes it very easy to blame or question God. I have not had that experience so I cannot speak to how one gets through such a difficult time. There are other examples in life where we blame God. I have a friend who lost his wife when their only child was a baby. He seemed to handle it by denying the existence of a God. I cannot relate to this either. My suggestion is to seek help/counseling from a trusted clergy member and to keep the lines of communication with God open through prayer and reading of Scripture. Attend healing services/seminars until the pain, which I can only imagine as beyond description, has subsided. I am not sure it ever goes away. I know that for me, having buried both of my parents, I still miss them. There are still many times I want to call my dad to ask him how to do something or to ask him to help me with a project. The pain of that is very much diminished, but is still present. It is just not debilitating. I do know that often times the pain of losing a loved one, such as a parent, is much worse when we live with the "I wish I had" syndrome. I wish I had spent more time with the loved one, I wish I had told him or her I loved them, etc. Anita's father died suddenly when we were in college. Just before he had died, the family went to Cuba (the border was still open) to visit friends. Her father had asked Anita if she wanted to go along, but her boss at the department store where she worked part time during school and full time during the summer, would not give her the time off. She elected to stay home and work. A week after they came home, her father committed suicide, apparently under the stress of financial problems. Years later, when we could not afford to go on a family vacation because we had loaned money to another family and then the engine in my truck had blown and had to be replaced, Anita became very upset when I said we just could not afford a vacation that year. The kind of upset and the intensity of her reaction to the situation were, in my opinion, way out of whack from her normal loving and accepting nature. In fact it started to become a rift between the two of us. While at work, during my lunch hour, I asked God to give me wisdom regarding the situation. What came to mind was her father's sudden death. I came home and suggested to Anita that she might want to pray about it to see if she could find the link between her strong reaction and her father's death. After praying she realized she had vowed that she would never miss another family vacation. After all she missed the last vacation her family had taken and then her father died.

What Anita did then was remarkable. She wrote a letter to her father sharing her pain at not being with them on that vacation. She also told her father in the letter how much she loved him and how much she missed him. She forgave him for leaving the family and she forgave God for letting him die. She then took the letter in a sealed envelope and placed in on a side altar in our Catholic Parish, which was her way of getting the letter delivered to her father. She was able to release the pain and we went on without the deep strife we were experiencing.

I have my own personal experience of needing to forgive God. Some people might laugh at this, but I think it is representative of what some people might go through and not even realize they are angry with God. I told you I am 6' 6" tall, and in the mid 1950's that was considered big, even for basketball players. When we moved from Long Island, to Cherry Valley, NY I was in the 7th grade and only eleven years old. My parents had started me in school a year earlier than most children because of my size. Well, when you move from the city to a farming community, one is not easily accepted by the locals. In fact it seemed that the farm boys would pick fights with me just to show they were stronger and tougher. Our coach (who was the gym teacher for grades K-12) had a practice during the long winter months of putting the boxing gloves on any boys who got into a fight, and have them box it out in front of the entire school. It seemed like I was in the ring with someone almost every week that winter, and not being strong like the kids who grew up on the farm, I usually lost. My father's view was that I had to learn to deal with it. Needless to say, it was quite humiliating. By the time the 8th grade came along, we had formed a junior high basketball team. I had gotten stronger, so the other boys not only stopped picking fights with me, but realized I was a pretty good asset to making a very promising basketball team. I was experiencing acceptance and that was important to me. Well we had several undefeated seasons in high school, and I managed to receive a scholarship to a division II school. When I got to college, back on Long Island, I did not play much but the other guys and some alumni saw my potential. By my junior year I was running with the first team, shooting 53% completion rate on my shots from the top of the key hole. Two days before the opening day, I broke my thumb, on my left hand. I am left handed. The coach told me how disappointed he was as he planned to put me in the starting lineup, and our team was rated one of the top teams in the northeast. That spring, while home on the farm I was pulling hay out of the hay mow when I pulled a muscle in my lower back and could no longer sustain running three hours a night at practice. I did not make the team my senior year. Between the injury my junior year and now my hurting back, I was crushed. To add insult to injury, at the end of the season, our school was selected to represent the USA against the Cuban National team on a tour of Cuba. I asked to be included, but was turned down. So what does this have to do with God? Years later, while going through inner healing, I was praying and asked God to show me the root of some emotional pain I was experiencing in my life at that time. In my prayer, in my imagination, Jesus led me back to the farm and into the hay mow, the place where I had hurt my back. We just sat there and finally I realized why He had led me there. I said to Jesus, "I must be angry with you for my getting hurt." Now, realize I was not conscious of any anger toward God, but He simply said "Yes I was angry with Him." I prayed a prayer to forgive Him and then asked for forgiveness for holding onto it for such a long time. The emotional pain I had been dealing with subsided. I can now see that it is probably good that my basketball career ended. When I started teaching, I wanted to coach basketball at the JR/SR high school where I had gotten a job as a math teacher. I was turned down, and

I am sure that not playing very much in college did not help the situation. Being turned down for the coaching job was one of the factors that led me to leave teaching and I ended up in computer programming. When I look back, I probably did not have the right emotional make up to coach, and I found that my true gift was in the area of using my logical mind. When God closes one door He opens up another. I just did not realize this at that time in my life.

Forgiveness of self is probably the hardest thing to do. It might just be one of the most important things one can and must do if one is to experience to any degree the depth of God's love for us. As a Catholic I cannot tell you how many times I went to confession, confessed my failures (sins), received absolution from the priest, and walked out still thinking I was a failure. Why is it so hard to do, to forgive ourselves? Let me throw out a few thoughts. The simple answer is that it comes along with our fallen nature. In the garden, man separated from God and the accuser took over and began to tell us how bad we were. This has been reinforced since our childhood in many of our homes where our parents reinforced that notion. Now I am not blaming my parents. The fact is, we were often told that we were loved for our good behavior, and not so loved for our not so good behavior. The main line churches in many ways also reinforced this. We had to earn God's love. We had to earn the right to go to heaven. The Catholic Church had venial and mortal sins, and still does in many of its practices. In fact deep down, I think one of the main reasons I did not go to church (I did not have God at the center of my life) was because I just saw myself as a person who could not live up to what was expected as the norm for earning God's love. My wife, Anita, is very self-disciplined but I am not. I have friends who are very self-disciplined. I just could not live up to the standard they set. Another way to put this is that my focus was on my failures and not on who I was as a person, the person God created me to be. I tried many times to put self-discipline in my life and always fell short of my expectations. To express it another way, I was sin conscious and could not seem to eliminate the sin from my life.

One of the side effects of not forgiving one's self is that we will never see ourselves as measuring up to be able to do God's work in our lives. We have this lie imbedded deep within us that all we need is to be perfect to do His work. God does not use perfect people. He uses people who believe Him and trust Him.

Going back to Matthew (22:35-40):

> *"You shall love the Lord your God with all your heart, with all your soul, and with all your mind."* [38] This is *the* first and great commandment. [39] And *the* second *is* like it: *You shall love your neighbor as yourself.* [40] On these two commandments hang all the Law and the Prophets.

Jesus said to love your neighbor as you love yourself. It is virtually impossible to love yourself if you cannot forgive yourself. Another way to put it is, you cannot give what you don't have. If you don't see yourself as loved and as loveable, it certainly limits how much you can love others.

I had to come to grips with a couple of things. You might even say they are the same thing. First I had to come to grips with the fact that Jesus died and while on the cross he forgave me for all of my sins. So I finally had to come to the mindset, once I believed he forgave and forgives my sins, then who am I to think I have the right to make me an exception to that fact? I AM FORGIVEN. The other part of this is to come to the following conclusion. Years ago there was a Catholic Lay Evangelist by the name of Charlie Osburn. Charlie is from the state of Florida, and he was given the title of Evangelist by his Bishop. Charlie traveled all over the USA and perhaps elsewhere preaching the Gospel. The term "Lay" means a person who is not ordained. His message, simply put, is to love one another. We went to hear him whenever he came to town and also when he was on TV. He often referred to us as children of God. We heard him preach dozens of times, and I heard clearly that we were children of God, but I never internalized it. It was something I understood, but never applied to my life in any real way. I even spoke with him on a number of visits and asked him to pray for me, because I had not yet arrived. He told me it was a process.

We were also doing healing seminars ourselves, and having people come to the house for prayers. During these years we saw many people healed, although most were inner healings. As time moved on, we lost our priests as, one died suddenly and another just got busy, so the ministry slowly waned. A few years later, a lady came all the way across town for prayers. I was not sure we had helped her, but to this day when we run into her she tells us how much our healing prayer sessions helped her. In any case she mentioned, at the time that she was also seeing a person who was internationally known in the church for her power of discernment. I was quite surprised, so I asked her if she meant the person of the same name who was from New York. She said yes, it was she and that she and her husband had retired to Phoenix.

I must digress for a moment. In 1980 when I was at my very worst with my depression, I had been reading books about healing and had learned from these books that there were gifts of the Holy Spirit that included words of knowledge, which in effect, as I understood it, were given to help one understand what in one's life needed to be healed. We decided to ask God to lead us to such a person. We ended up at the church of a very holy and gifted priest who labored in the healing ministry. I asked him if he had the gift of knowledge to tell me what the root of my problem was. His response was that at that time there were maybe four people in the Charismatic Movement in the Catholic Church in the USA who had that gift. He mentioned the name of a person from NY. I asked the priest what I needed to do to go see her. He told me that there was probably a four year waiting list to get to see her. Since I was, among other things, suicidal at that point, I could not wait four years. I decided that God would have to heal me without her help.

Since she was now in Phoenix, some 15 or 20 years later, I got her phone number and set up an appointment to see her. My reason was that I was starting to struggle with depression again. When I went to see her, we talked for a few minutes, and then she suddenly went into what I would call a trance. She told me I had a spirit of rejection that she could deliver but that God told her not to deliver it. She said the spirit came from childhood issues, but that was not important. She said God wanted me to learn to love myself, and that when I did learn to love myself the spirit would leave on its own. Furthermore, when I learned to love myself God, would restore the healing ministry and it would be more powerful than ever.

So now the task became learning to love myself. I tried to do that and every time I failed (sinned) I went back to seeing myself as a loser. We started to watch Joel Osteen on Sunday mornings before we went to Mass. It seemed like there was a period of 10 to 15 weeks where Joel would say, in one form or another, that we were God's children. I don't know when it happened, but one day I think I finally got it. I am a child of God. I am not perfect. If I were perfect, I would not need God. God made me as I am. He loves me just as I am, and if it is good enough for God, it is more than good enough for me. I accept the fact that I fail, I ask for forgiveness when I do, and have learned to love the person God created.

Chapter 12
How to Forgive

The question which must be asked is, "How does one forgive?" A question related to this is, "How do I know when I have truly forgiven?" Let's talk about these two questions. But before we do, I want to talk about what I observed in my life with regard to forgiveness.

Prior to my bout with depression (described in an earlier chapter) I would simply decide to forgive someone or something and I thought I was done with it. Then I started to notice a pattern, particularly with people with whom I was close. I would often find myself saying things like, "That's the tenth time you did that." (Even though I thought I had forgiven all the other times). Or I would say or think, "He/she always does that." I also noticed that the emotional level of what I was feeling seemed to increase. Another pattern would be to avoid certain subjects or avoid contact with a person who hurt me in some form. What we came to realize is that it is not necessarily the big hurts that drag us down, but it is often all the little hurts that accumulate. These do as much, or more, damage. Furthermore, it is not just the things that are said or done to us. We can get just as hurt by lots of little things. I have noticed over time, for example, that in many families the wife/mother seems to carry far more than her share of the load, often being ignored or unappreciated for her work. It is very easy for a person to become slowly hurt and angry by such behavior, which is more common than we realize.

When my psychiatrist told me he thought forgiveness was

a bunch of BS, it made me stop and think. The conclusion I came to was, in many cases, my experience of forgiveness, giving or receiving, seemed to be of little use. What I slowly realized was that I had never entered into prayer to forgive someone. For me, that was the missing element.

In Luke 6: 27-33:

> [27] But to you who hear I say, *love your enemies, do good to those who hate you,* [28] *bless those who curse you, pray for those who mistreat you.* [29] To the person who strikes you on one cheek, offer the other one as well, and from the person who takes your cloak, do not withhold even your tunic. [30] Give to everyone who asks of you, and from the one who takes what is yours do not demand it back. [31] Do to others as you would have them do to you. [32] For if you love those who love you, what credit is that to you? Even sinners love those who love them. [33] And if you do good to those who do good to you, what credit is that to you? Even sinners do the same.

In this passage and in the words following, Jesus tells us how to relate to people. When I read Luke 6:27 and following, I began to pray for those who hurt me, and I also asked God to bless them. When I began to do this the small hurts went away quickly and I stopped keeping score. The bigger hurts often took longer. My wife and I prayed for years for the man who attacked Linda. I also prayed for years to forgive my mother for her lack of affection, etc. Over the years we have come to believe that we will meet the man who attacked Linda when we are in heaven. I can tell you that this is far better (and healthier) than keeping hatred and anger in my heart. I must admit that the acid test would be to meet him face to face while here on earth. That has not happened. At one point I wanted to write to him while he was in jail, but Linda was not ready for that, so I dropped the idea.

I now make it a practice to bless someone who offends me or disturbs my peace. For example, as I drive a little slower each year it is not unusual for someone to become impatient with me and either honk their horn, or race by me, sometimes flashing half of a peace sign my way. I used to flash the same half back at them, but I have replaced that with praying for God to bless them. Since I am of the Catholic faith I will often visually make the sign of the cross as I pray the blessing. One day my son-in-law and I were returning a movie to the rental store. Rather than pull into a parking spot, I stopped behind the parked cars while he jumped out to deposit the movie in the return slot. Well, a driver in the car behind me became impatient, pressed down on the horn, and sped around me toward a parking spot. As he passed me, I made the sign of the cross and prayed a blessing. He jumped out of his car and started racing toward me looking very angry. However, by the time he got to my truck, he looked at me and said, "Please forgive me for my impatience."

Sometimes when I find it particularly difficult to forgive someone, I ask Jesus to allow me to see the person as he sees them.

I want to make one other point. I discovered that at times. I need to have the feelings I am experiencing validated before I can move on to forgiveness. Let me give you an example. I found myself unable to forgive the priests who molested children. While no one in my immediate family was molested I know people whose children were molested. I found it to be a pain that I could not shed. When I would talk to my wife and more than a few other people about my pain, they generally brushed it off saying something like, "They are men and they will fail, so let go of it." I finally thought there was something wrong with me that I could not let go of this deep pain and the anger that went along with it. I finally decided to go to a priest in confession and confess my anger as a sin. He told me my anger towards those priests was not a sin, that I had every right to be angry and that, quite frankly, he was worried about the people who were denying any anger. He also told me that if I did not let go of the anger it would slowly destroy me, which it was already doing. He even gave me the name of a counselor who I might want to see for some help. Just having someone listen to my pain, and validating me as a person were enough for me to move on. Please don't get me wrong. In no way do I condone the actions of those men or anyone else who has engaged in taking advantage of innocent children. What I do know is that staying angry will only destroy me, and consequently those whom I love the most. I have to believe that God, in all of His love and in His wisdom, will apply justice to the situation(s).

So how do we know when we have forgiven someone? The word of God tells us in 1 Thessalonians 5:16-19

> [16] Rejoice always. [17] Pray without ceasing. [18] In all circumstances give thanks, for this is the will of God for you in Christ Jesus. [19] Do not quench the Spirit.

When we can thank God for what has happened in our lives, I believe we have reached a pretty good level of forgiveness. Let me be very clear. We are not thanking God for what happened to us, but rather we are thanking him because He is working and has worked within the situation. Remember earlier, how we talked about Romans 8:28 where God turns all things together for good for those who love Him. We also said in 1 John 5:3 that the love of God is to keep His commandments. Well, it is God's will that we give thanks in all things. I have found that the practice of giving thanks in all things produces a grateful heart in me.

Chapter 13

Asking For Forgiveness

Let's discuss the act of asking for forgiveness. In Matthew 5:23-25 Jesus tells us:

> Therefore if you bring your gift to the altar, and there remember that your brother has something against you leave your gift there before the altar, and go your way. First be reconciled to your brother, and then come and offer your gift.

How often have we had a fight with someone, usually in the family, and then gone to church (the altar) and pretended like nothing was wrong. In the ministry we have run into untold numbers of people where someone has not talked to a brother, or sister, or parent or child for years. It's no wonder the church is not believed by the world. Jesus says very clearly, "Go first and be reconciled, then come to church."

I like to give examples as the way to teach what happens when we try to live out what God's word is telling us to do. Perhaps the best example I can give you happened when our daughter Linda was attacked the second time.

We got the call at three in the morning but this time it was from our third daughter, Cathy. I told her to find Lisa, our second daughter (they were all attending the University of Arizona) and for the three of them to come home. When we got home from Mass that morning and when Linda and Cathy woke up, one of the things I asked them was, "Where was Lisa?

They said they couldn't find her so they left a message for her and came home without her. I accepted that in light of the fact that it was a "party" weekend at the U of A and they did not all hang out together all the time. By Saturday evening Lisa had not checked in with family so I decided to call the Tucson police as I was afraid something bad might have happened to her also. As I picked up the phone to call, one of the girls said, "Don't bother calling the police. We know where Lisa is". They went on to tell us that Lisa had gone to Mexico, with friends for the weekend. I got a bit upset that they had lied to me and that Lisa had not told us she was heading for Mexico. Furthermore, Lisa was a nursing student and we had gotten her a car to help her get around Tucson to her various hospital assignments and by now I was sure she probably took the car to Mexico without purchasing insurance. One could say I was quite upset.

Since Linda had been attacked I also wanted to be sure she had some support from her siblings and I wanted to discuss the whole thing in case Linda did need more support. I wanted the other two girls to buy into the possibility of moving in with Linda if she needed it. Consequently I called for a family meeting the following Saturday evening, asking all three girls to come home then.

During the week I prayed asking God how to handle the situation. I asked for wisdom regarding whether or not Linda needed support from her sisters and for wisdom as to how to approach the Mexico trip by Lisa and the other two covering up for their sister.

All week long whenever I prayed I heard God tell me I was to ask for forgiveness. I heard nothing else. So I would ask again and I would hear the same message. I began to wonder if God's answer was really meant for someone else. I knew better but could not see the connection to my problem, that being my needing wisdom as to how to approach the whole mess.

When Saturday evening came we sat around the table and I asked each family member to talk about what had happened to Linda and where they were with it. It turns out we ended up going by age, with Christopher being the youngest and going first. When it came to my turn, I prayed that God would give me the words I needed to say. I said something like this, "Apparently over the years I have treated you such that you did not trust me enough to tell me the truth about what was going on, with Lisa going to Mexico and you other two hiding that fact from me. So I need to ask for forgiveness for all the times I have not been the father you needed me to be." Chris and Cathy said they forgave me but Lisa and Linda unloaded with lots of angry words. Then they both stomped out of the room. I sat there stunned. I prayed and I told God, "This is not what I was hoping for." I just sat there stunned. I looked at Anita and she said something like, "Well you asked for it."

An hour or two later one of the girls came back and said she was praying and that she forgave me. We hugged and cried together. The next morning the other came to me and said she had spent a long time praying and that she too forgave me. More hugs and tears.

The whole family then agreed we, including us, Mom and Dad, needed to be accountable to each other and to let each other know when one of us going someplace other than the normal routine places. To this day, even though all of them are married, we still try let each other know where we will be going. I say try, because they each have their own families and their attention is in that direction. It was another lesson in learning that doing things God's way is the only way to go.

I want to add a couple of examples that helped drive the point home. Another time when I was upset about what one of the girls had done, I was directed by God, after asking for wisdom, to take my problem to the priest in the sacrament of reconciliation. I won't go into details but I actually thought she was the one who should go to confession. I could not understand why God was directing me to go, but I was obedient. In the course of talking to the priest, I mentioned I had asked my daughter for forgiveness for my outburst of anger toward the situation. The priest became overwhelmed, that I, as a father would ask my children for forgiveness. He said that in his 40 plus years as a priest he personally had never heard of a father asking his children for forgiveness. I wonder if that does not speak volumes about what might be going on in family life.

Another time, Anita and I were speaking on the subject of parenting at the Newman Center at the University of Arizona. When we had finished, the nun who had invited us to speak approached us and said that what we said was absolutely amazing. We asked what she meant. Her response was that we had no idea about the number of speakers she has had at the University speaking on the subject of parenting, many of whom were PhDs and who had published books on parenting. Never had she heard anyone even suggest that a father (or mother) ask his/her children for forgiveness. I asked "Was that wrong?" Her reply was' "No, it is so right on and very much needed in family life."

Let's discuss another scripture regarding the subject of asking for forgiveness. In Matthew 7:1-5 Jesus said the following:

¹ Judge not, that you be not judged. ² For with what judgment you judge, you will be judged; and with the measure you use, it will be measured back to you. *³ And why do you look at the speck in your brother's eye, but do not consider the plank in your own eye? ⁴ Or how can you say to your brother, Let me remove the speck from your eye; and look, a plank is in your own eye? ⁵ Hypocrite!*

Let's focus on versus 3 and 4. I believe what Jesus is telling us here is that we are to look at our own actions first. He knows that we are built with plenty of opportunity to mess up a relationship. So we are to stop looking at the other person and his or her actions and change our own behavior. This is, in my opinion, particularly true in love relationships and possibly most apparent in the husband and wife relationship.

I think Romans 2:1 sums up and supplements the above very well.

"Therefore, you are without excuse, every one of you who passes judgment. For by the standard by which you judge another you condemn yourself, since you, the judge, do the very same things."

I believe what this verse is telling us is that the reason you can see the fault in another person is due to the fact that you know that fault, because you have it as well.

This was best driven home to me when I was upset about a friend who was in a sexual relationship without being married to that person. My judgment was strong and I expressed my thoughts aloud one day. Anita said that I should not judge another person like that. I asked God to show me why I was so upset, especially in light of Romans 2:1. My defense with God was that I was not in such a relationship. As I quieted down to listen, God showed my patterns of deceit in my life such as sneaking ice cream from the refrigerator after Anita had gone to bed. He showed me that my un-repented deceit was the root of my judgment toward my friend. When I repented, I stopped judging my friend. I am not saying what he was doing was OK. What I am saying is that I was able to let go and let God do the judging.

Chapter 14
Healing Testimonies in Our Family

───────────◯───────────

I want to take a little time to share some of the healings that we have experienced. Some will be stories of healings within my family and some will be healings of others; Some will be what is called inner healing and others will be about physical healing. I am not going to get into a discussion about which is more important (inner healing or physical healing), I simply want to give witness to what God has done.

In my journey of coming out of the deep depression which had hospitalized me, I had many healings. I want to mention just two of them, as I believe it would have taken years of therapy to even get close to the situations.

When we took Linda over to California to the healing workshop presented by the Linn brothers, they offered inner healing prayer just before dinner. I had had a very powerful day up until then and I knew we wanted to have dinner and be sure we got back for the session on physical healing that evening, so I thought I would skip the inner healing prayers. Two things happened when I said I would skip the prayers. First, Anita got quite upset. She said this was one of the reasons we came here, for me to experience healing. At the same time my friend Al said he thought he needed to go for prayers. I thought if he needed prayers, then maybe I needed them as well, so over I went to where the healing teams were. I ended up being prayed for by a husband and wife team. When I told them why I was there, suffering from depression, the husband said something like, "We'll take him on a trip." I did not know what that meant but decided to go along with it. The wife stood behind me and began to pray in what sounded like tongues and the husband directed me in a prayer experience using my imagination. He had me describe a favorite place and I mentioned going deer hunting on the farm where I lived as a teenager. He asked me if there were any caves near there. I told him I remembered a cave-like place where a tree had been uprooted. I would sometimes sit in this hole to get out of the cold wind. Why I picked that place, I have no idea. He asked me to use my imagination and to pick up a stick which would be my light; that I was to take the stick and tap the dirt on the side of the hill, and imagine there was a cave behind the dirt. He told me to enter the cave, and to believe that Jesus was there with me. It was kind of bizarre but I went along with it and clung to the faith that Jesus was with me. He said at the end of the cave I would enter a room. I told him I was at the end of the cave and there was no room there. I just wanted to get out of there. He asked me to trust Jesus and in my imagination to use the stick to tap at the end of the cave again. When I did that I can only say that I found myself in what seemed like a free fall, kind of a time tunnel and I was very frightened. He assured me that Jesus was with me and that I had entered a room and to describe the room. I told him I was in a hospital room and I was all alone. Again he told me to see, in faith, that Jesus was with me. While I could not see Jesus in my imagination, I decided to accept that he was there. He asked how old I was and I said that I was 6 years old. I was in the hospital and I was quarantined as they thought I had polio. He told me to imagine my parents there as well and I said they would not come, or they could not come. He said Jesus would bring them to me. I saw my father, but told the husband that my mother would not come. He said, "No, Jesus would get her, and I saw my mother wanting to reach out to me, but did not know how. While all this was going on, waves of loneliness were pouring out of me as I sat there and cried away the pain.

When I was 6 years old, I was placed in quarantine for almost a week while they tested me for polio. My parents would come to the window of my room every evening and even sent in ice cream for me to eat, but they could not come in. It was during World War II, so my father could only come in the evening and my mother did not drive. I remember when I came home at the end of the ordeal, my father had traded gasoline rationing stamps for meat rationing stamps and the family celebrated my return home with a steak dinner (something we did not have during the war). When I left the prayer team I had what I can only explain as an out of body experience. To this day I don't know what the experience means, but as I walked up the aisle of the auditorium in which we were, I felt like my spirit had left my body and was bouncing off the ceiling. When we got outside heading toward our car, Linda was out there having a cigarette. As we walked toward the car she said, "Earth to Dad: come down, you look like you are 20 feet tall." As we walked under some pine trees, she said I looked like I was up in the pine trees, which was exactly what I was experiencing. I don't know what all of that out of body stuff meant, but I can only say my anxiety level dropped dramatically from that prayer experience. God is amazing.

The second major inner healing I had was perhaps even more bizarre than the one I just described. But it had an incredible affect on me and on my relationship with Anita. We attended a healing workshop in Portland Oregon, which was put on by a Jesuit priest, Fr Van Houton S.J., and he worked with a female Christian therapist whose name I do not remember. She, the therapist, gave a talk showing how children can experience both emotional and physical wounds while still in their mother's womb. At the end of the talk, she prayed for healing for anyone in the room who had experienced such wounds. During her prayer I began to cry as I experienced very deep healing. Specifically, waves of rejection poured out of me as she prayed, and I saw flashes of my life pass by, as if on a movie screen, when I wished I had been a girl instead of being a boy in order to please my parents. Some explanation is in order.

When my mother became pregnant with me my parents knew that I would be their last child due to my mother's health. Since I have an older brother, they must have expressed their desire to have a girl to go along with a boy. I have no conscious memory of this and in fact, just a few weeks before the healing took place, I had asked my parents to talk about the memories of having me as my birthday present from them. I was in my forties when this took place. They told me they had hoped for a girl but they more than demonstrated how pleased they were to have me. They talked at length about not only my birth, but the joys of raising both my brother and me.

In both of the above healing experiences, I cannot imagine how much therapy would have been needed to get to the same points. In fact I cannot imagine it ever happening without the power of the Holy Spirit.

In September of 1963, I transferred from the east coast to Phoenix, Arizona within the General Electric Company. GE had its headquarters for its computer business in Phoenix. Anita and I had one child and she was pregnant with our second child. Moving to Phoenix, we believed, afforded us the chance to buy a home, which we could not afford on the east coast at the time. In late November, my new boss called a meeting to tell us she had decided to step down from management and that we would be assigned to other managers as part of a general reorganization. I was told I would be assigned to work for Mr. A (obviously not his name) and that he would be contacting me. A few days later, an internal news letter came out in which Mr. A had announced his new organization and my name was not included. I went to my boss who immediately went to see her boss, Mr. B, to see what happened. She came back and told me to go see Mr. B immediately. Mr. B then told me that Mr. A refused to include me in his new organization because he did not know me, nor did anyone he trusted know me. I never was interviewed by Mr. A. Mr. B then told me he had no position for me, so he gave me two weeks to find a job somewhere in the plant or I would be laid off. I walked out of his office stunned only to learn that President John F. Kennedy had been shot and killed that morning. I received permission to go home early which I did. When I got home, I tried to tell Anita that I had lost my job, but the news about the president was so consuming that we just spent the entire weekend watching what transpired. When I left for work on Monday morning Anita said to me, "What do you mean you have no job? They just transferred us out here. What are we going to do?"

I found a job that next week in engineering, working on a new large scale computer that GE was developing. It turned out to be a blessing for me as I found my niche doing operating system development. Now let's fast forward some 18 years. I had had my nervous breakdown and was in the process of recovering. On the day President Reagan was shot, I went home that evening and mentioned to Anita that I was not feeling well and that I was developing a headache. Anita was alarmed by the statement. So she must have sensed something in me that I did not sense. In any case, I went to bed early that evening, and when I woke up in the morning, my back was hurting so badly that I could not even move. I took pain pills and muscle relaxants, but could not get out of bed. On the third day, I forced myself to get up and go to work despite the fact that I could barely walk. That day at work, I was walking slowly down the hall when a friend stopped me to ask about the pain I was experiencing. We happened to be standing just outside the offices where I had been told I had no job 18 years earlier. As we talked about my back, I closed my eyes and asked Jesus to show me the root of my back pain. In my imagination I saw the faces of Mr. A and Mr. B, mentioned above. I prayed a simple prayer to forgive both of them and asked God to bless them, wherever they were. Within 3-5 seconds all the pain in my back was gone.

I had experienced a major healing with regard to my back a few years earlier more so than what I just described. I want to mention this because in the example above, one can see where past hurts not truly dealt with can cause problems somewhere in our bodies at a later time. In my case, my back seemed to be the weak spot that was targeted. When I injured my back in college and could no longer play basketball, my back problems persisted. At one point my orthopedic surgeon ran some tests and told me I had a deteriorating (or bulging disc) that might someday need surgery. During the time I was recovering from depression there was a man named John Kojanis who went from parish to parish teaching scripture and healing the afflicted. I went to see him every time he came into town hoping to receive more healing. Anita even asked, "How often must we go to see him?" I told her I would go until I no longer needed healing. On his third or fourth visit to Phoenix, I went with a friend of mine to hear him teach again. When he began to pray for those who needed healing he asked those near us to lay hands on the afflicted area. My friend Bill placed his hands on my back. During the prayer, I felt what I thought were Bill's hands wrapped around my spinal cord, kneading the bulging disc back into place. When we finished I had absolutely no pain and as I put my own hands on my back I realized Bill could not have had his fingers around my spinal cord. It was a work of the Holy Spirit. I was so excited, I went back to jogging a couple of miles the next day and lo and behold my back hurt again. I eventually saw my orthopedic surgeon who ran tests and told me my disc problem had disappeared. He concluded my back problems were now muscular and suggested that I do lots of muscle strengthening exercises. I must admit I am not very disciplined in this area, so I have learned to kind of live with occasional back pain, some caused by things like what I talked about above, namely unmitigated anger, some caused by very tight hamstring muscles and some caused by my being macho and lifting more than I should. One of the messages in the above example is that God did not heal my back the first three or four times I heard John Kojanis teach. So often if people do not get healed immediately they assume God does not want to heal them. Why I did not get healed sooner, I do not know. However, if and when I need healing I keep seeking the Lord. I think it is interesting that people will go to the doctor over and over again and, even try different doctors, but quite often they will seek the Lord only once, if at all, and then give up.

I have one other story that I think is significant. I mentioned in an example earlier in the book about having trouble forgiving the priests who had molested children. I had an even bigger struggle forgiving those bishops who, over the years, attempted to cover up the scandal. Anita was reading a book called "Left to Tell" which was about a woman from Rwanda who survived the holocaust in her country. Most of her family was murdered. Anita got a copy of the book from the local library for me to read while we were going to spend a long weekend at a resort in Mexico. I sat by the pool and while reading the book, I became overwhelmed by the woman's faith. I am normally a slow reader and do not read for long periods, but I could not put the book down. While reading the book, I sensed a prompting by the Holy Spirit. So I put the book down and began to pray. I heard the Holy Spirit implore me to forgive the bishops who had covered up the scandal. The Holy Spirit told me they were men who were trying to do what was best, but, in many cases did not have the faith required to "do the right thing". I saw in the spirit, if you will, men who were weak in their faith and I became compassionate towards them. Again, as I said earlier with forgiving the priests, I do not condone what they did, but my being angry did not help anyone. If anything, my anger was hurting me and thus those closest to me. My own opinion is that the leaders of the church who did any form of cover up need to publicly ask forgiveness of the people, but that is not up to me.

A week or two later I had a blood test for my annual physical. When I was in the doctor's office actually having the physical, I was telling him how I had forgiven the bishops for the cover up. My doctor's reply was that my cholesterol level had dropped from high to a perfect score and he was going to ask me what I had done to make that happen. He believed my act of forgiving the bishops played a large role in lowering my cholesterol. My doctor is of the Jewish faith and here I was witnessing to him about Jesus and he said to me he wanted to see me in six months. I asked him if there was something wrong and his reply was that he loved to hear my stories and he wanted me to come in to tell him more on a more frequent basis. He of course was joking about the frequency of visits, but he was not joking about hearing the witness I gave him when I went to see him.

I want to mention one more area for healing which can be behavior changing, and that is making vows. The following scripture from Matthew, chapter 5 talks about vows.

> [33] Again you have heard that it was said to the men of old, "You shall not swear falsely, but shall perform to the Lord what you have sworn." [34] But I say to you, "Do not swear at all, either by heaven, for it is the throne of God, [35] or by the earth, for it is his footstool, or by Jerusalem, for it is the city of the great King. [36] And do not swear by your head, for you cannot make one hair white or black. [37] Let what you say be simply "Yes' or 'No"; anything more than this comes from evil."

A friend had called and told me about a teaching he and his wife had heard regarding making vows. In simplest terms one can become bound by a vow one makes. The above scripture tells us not to make vows but to say yes when we mean yes and no when we mean no.

I took in what he told me and I sat down one evening to pray about any vows I might have made in my life aside from vowing to take my wife for life. Two vows came to mind. Let me talk about them.

When Anita and I were dating I got the sense that my then mother-in-law to be had three things she would rather see in her future son-in-law. One was that I would be of the Catholic Faith, which I was not; one was that I would be Italian, again which I was not, and the third was that I would be rich, and that was not the case either. When

Anita and I got married anyway, she told me shortly after the wedding that I could call her "Mother" if I wished. In a way it was her way of saying "Welcome to the family." But I was tainted in my thinking by what I just mentioned about her evaluation of me, so under my breath I said, "I will never call you Mother." As time went on and I got over what I thought had been her evaluation of me, I wanted to start calling her Mother, but much like the Fonz on Happy Days, the word mother just got stuck in my throat. So I never called her mother.

The second vow I made apparently came from seeing my parents fight about money as I grew up. I am shortening the story but we did not have very much money and I saw my mother go to the Newberry's store on her lunch hour on a fairly regular basis and buy things we simply did not need. This, and things like it, often caused discord between my parents with regard to money. The Lord showed me in prayer that I had made a vow to never spend money frivolously.

The vow to not spend money frivolously carried over into Anita's and my marriage. I could not even except gifts from her that I thought we did not need. One year for my birthday, Anita got me a CB radio for my pickup truck. CB radios were big in those days, well before cell phones. I made her take it back. I could never allow myself to buy Anita things like jewelry, even though she loves jewelry.

When the Lord showed me these two vows, I repented of having done so, and it just so happened that one of the priests from our parish was coming over for dinner the next day. When he got to our house I asked him if we could go into the other room where I asked him to hear my confession. I explained where I was coming from with regard to the scripture and after asking for forgiveness I also asked if he would lay hands and break any power over me that might have come from the evil one. When he did pray, I felt like chains that were wrapped around my chest were breaking and I knew I was free from the vows. For my penance he asked me to reconcile with my mother-in-law. I would rather have been asked to do something else, but here also I knew the spirit of God was working.

It turns out my mother-in-law was also coming over for dinner that evening, so when she got to our house, I took her aside and asked for forgiveness that I had never called her Mother. She forgave me immediately and said that she had come to like being called Nana, since we had all four of our children by then. I will have to say going through the process of asking for forgiveness drew me closer to her.

Breaking the other vow was also a huge step in my journey. I became freed from not being able to spend money and have since allowed both Anita and myself to show our love to each other and to our children and to others. I have bought lots of nice jewelry for Anita, I became willing to send my children to do things like study abroad, I have become generous in giving to many people and many causes. In fact I would readily state that we have become financially blessed, even though by US standards we are far from rich.

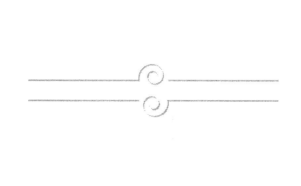

Chapter 15
Healing Testimonies Outside Our Family

Let me tell you about a few of the healings with which we have been involved outside of our family. Let me begin with one of my favorite healings, although as I say that, I have many favorite healings because of how people were affected. I have come to realize what an awesome God we have. Also I think you will see that there is no one method to healing. Basically, one has to follow the lead of the Holy Spirit. In fact when we first began to pray over people who came to our house for healing, I would ask God to let next the person coming have the same problem as the last, so I would know how to pray. He did not do that. I quickly learned that my part was to become sensitive to the prompting of the Holy Spirit. Also, I hope you come to know more deeply than ever, how incredibly good, loving and merciful God is.

Anita and I were in another city giving our Forgiveness and Healing workshop at a parish there. As I mentioned it in an earlier chapter, we start Saturday morning with a talk about forgiveness followed by an extensive prayer experience where people are led to forgive anyone and everyone who has hurt them. Later in the afternoon we have a foot washing experience where one can ask someone for forgiveness. In this experience, if that person is not there, then they can ask someone to "stand in" for him or her. For example if I wanted to ask my dad for forgiveness and he is no longer alive, I would ask someone at the workshop to stand in for him.

There were between 100 to 150 people attending the workshop so I did not get to recognize everyone there. During the foot washing, a lady approached me and asked if I would wash her feet. Since I did not know her I asked who she wanted me to stand in for. She asked me to be her child. Then she asked me to forgive her for aborting me (her child). I was stunned by her request, but I told her I forgave her and that the Jesus in my heart forgave her. As I poured water over her foot she cried and cried and cried. I held her in my arms and simply let her cry. As she calmed down, I asked her if she was Roman Catholic and she said, "Yes." I told her the church teaches that this needs to be taken to the Sacrament of Reconciliation. She told me she had gone three times but that this was the first time she felt cleansed. That night at the closing Mass I can only tell you that even her facial features had changed. She seemed to be filled with life.

About a year later we were at a University in the same city preparing to present our workshop at the Newman Center there. This same lady walked in to register for the workshop and asked me if I remembered her. How would I ever forget? She then went on to tell me that she had not been in attendance at the workshop the previous year. She told me that on Saturday afternoon she was walking across the church parking lot when the Holy Spirit directed her to come into the building where we were doing the workshop. I got two messages from that. The first was that God wants to set us free from whatever has us bound no matter what we have done in our lives. The second message was more for Anita and me. We came to realize that, unlike what we had thought, someone did not need to hear us talk about forgiveness in order to have a meaningful experience at our workshop. It was God's work, not ours. It was a real lesson in humility for us.

Another example was when we got a call one Sunday evening from a friend we knew through Marriage Encounter. She asked if we could pray with her brother who had stopped at their house to tell her that he was leaving his wife and family to seek employment in another state. He said there was too much anger in the house due to his wife's drinking. We, of course said, "Yes." So the next night she and her husband brought her brother to our house. While Anita was getting some refreshments for everyone, he started to tell me that the only problem was the previously mentioned anger in the house. He said that he and his wife had gone on a Marriage Encounter weekend and that it did not work for them. He went on to say that he did not believe in touchy feely stuff, that he had not gone to church in the past 25 years or so, that he was an ex-marine who did not show his emotions, and that we had one night to solve this anger problem in the house or he was leaving. We decided we would simply pray over him and we invited his sister and brother-in-law to do the same. While praying, I was moved to start praying at his conception and for healing while in his mother's womb, during the actual birth process etc. At one point Anita leaned over and said he was sniffling so I told her to hand him a tissue. It was allergy season and I thought he might be dealing with allergies. When Anita gave him the tissue she whispered again to me to tell me he was actually weeping. I decided to end the prayer right there and let him weep. His sister than told me it was interesting that I had prayed for a longer amount of time when praying for what happened during his birth. She went on to say that when he was born he had lots of sores on his head and it must have been a painful birth experience. I thought that was an interesting observation. We talked quietly for about 30 minutes while this ex-marine who did not display emotions wept. We made a date for them to come back the next week and they left for home which was 30 to 40 minutes away. He wept all the way home. When he got home he told his wife where he had been, he told her he was going back to church, he wanted her to come with him, and that he was going back to our house next week. He hoped she would join him in this.

His wife did come with him the following week, and needless to say, she was very nervous, not knowing what to expect. We told her we were simply going to pray over her husband and she could join us or just observe. She chose to sit on the floor next to the chair where he was sitting and simply put her head on his lap. When we, Anita and I and his sister and brother-in-law, began to pray she started weeping. She wept for the rest of the evening and apparently experienced great healing. Isn't our God a wonderful God?

This time when we prayed over him I discerned a strong resistance by evil spirits. I was led to stop praying and to discuss what I was sensing with him. He said they had a number of friends who were Satan worshippers and that he knew deep inside they needed to sever the friendships. He also said there were weird things going on in their house that he believed were connected to these friends. I then asked if they were in full communion with the church. In other words were they receiving communion? His answer was that they had been away from the church for over 25 years, and he just did not want to face a priest in the Sacrament of Reconciliation. We gave them the name of a priest who knew about our ministry and suggested they contact him. We assured them that he would welcome them home when they went. I told them I did not want to deal with the evil spirits until they had done so. It took a while but they called on a Sunday and told me that they had gone to the priest the day before and that the two of them wept as they walked down the aisle to receive communion. They came over one more time for prayer and the evil spirits were gone. Their marriage was healed, they added to the size of their family by having more children, and he became a successful business man running his own business.

Another example took place when we got a call one evening from a lady who said she had trouble sleeping and that she also had trouble eating so she was losing weight. The reason was that her husband had left her and was living with a younger woman. She came over hoping to receive counseling. We don't really counsel as we had long before realized we are not qualified as counselors. We told her we would pray with her. When she got to our house we listened to her story and could easily feel her pain. We prayed over her and then told her she needed to forgive and to pray for her husband. See Luke 6 versus 27 and on. She told us she thought we were crazy but said she would go home and pray for her husband, asking God to bless him. We also gave her a tape to listen to which contained a talk we give on the subject of forgiveness. She came back a week or two later, saying that she was sleeping a little better but was still in great pain. We prayed over her again and told her she needed to forgive the woman and to ask God to bless the woman her husband was living with. She said she thought we were really crazy, but agreed to do as we suggested. She called a week or two later to tell us that her husband had come home unexpectedly asking for forgiveness, and to rebuild the marriage. She apparently told him she thought he had a problem with alcohol abuse. He agreed to seek help in that area. This occurred many years ago and we know they are still happily married today.

Here is one more story about inner healing. We have very close friends in another city who probably know more about marriage than any couple we know personally. One weekend we had attended a wedding of one of their children, and late Sunday afternoon after everyone had left and we were getting ready to head for the airport to go home, the wife said that we needed to talk. She asked her husband to tell us what he was planning to do. He told us he had been seeing a counselor for some emotional problems he was dealing with, and that the counselor told him his next step should be to leave his wife and live alone while he dealt with his problems. We were stunned. We also did not have much time. Besides, what could we tell them that they did not already know? We said that we wanted to pray over each of them individually. So we prayed over the wife first and she indicated that she was experiencing some peace. When we prayed over the husband, I told some evil spirit to "dry up". As soon as the words came out of my mouth I thought, "Why did I say that?" That seemed stupid to me. When we finished praying we asked what he had experienced and he told us that when I told the evil spirit to dry up, his mouth went bone dry. He asked what we thought that meant. We, of course, had no idea. We then had to hustle to get to the airport to catch our plane. We did not hear from them for a few weeks, so I called them and the wife answered. After exchanging pleasantries, I asked, what happened with her husband and his plan to leave her? She apologized that she had not called us, but she went on to say that the evening we prayed over them he began to talk about their situation. When he started talking, he simply cried out a lot of pain and his emotions were healed. His reason for leaving was also gone. Praise God!

Here are some examples of physical healing. Some friends came to visit us a couple of years ago. The husband was having trouble breathing. I thought he had walking pneumonia or some such thing. In any case, he went home and saw his doctor the next day. He was told that he had some kind of infection in his esophagus, the infection was not curable, and he would have to be on breathing treatments for the rest of his life. When he told me this over the phone, I gave him two scriptures to read and to pray about. One was Psalm 103 versus 3 and 4 which states, "He removes all our iniquities and heals all our diseases". I also gave him 1 Cor 2:5 which says "that your faith not be in the wisdom of men, but rather in the power of God".

The next day I called him and talked to him about the following scripture in Matthew 7.

> [14] And when they came to the crowd, a man came up to him and kneeling before him said, [15] "Lord, have mercy on my son, for he is an epileptic and he suffers terribly; for often he falls into the fire, and often into the water. [16] And I brought him to your disciples, and they could not heal him." [17] And Jesus answered, *"O faithless and perverse generation, how long am I to be with you? How long am I to bear with you? Bring him here to me."* [18] And Jesus rebuked him, and the demon came out of him, and the boy was cured instantly. [19] Then the disciples came to Jesus privately and said, "Why could we not cast it out?" [20] He said to them, *"Because of your little faith. For truly, I say to you, if you have faith as a grain of mustard seed, you will say to a mountain, "Move from here to there," and it will move; and nothing will be impossible to you."*

I specifically talked about the last part of verse 20, namely speaking to the mountain of his medical condition. I told him that he needed to speak to the condition every day, even 4 or 5 times a day telling the condition it had no right to be in his body and that it was to leave. I told him the condition would resist but he was to not lose heart, rather stay in faith that God heals every sickness and that it is by His power that it gets done. I told my friend to stay in faith. He apparently did so because when I called back a few weeks later he had gone to the doctor and his condition had been healed.

Another friend brought her niece over one night because she was suffering from Lupus. Before she got there I was reading various scriptures on healing and before we prayed over her I read those scriptures to her. She just seemed to be drinking in the Word. We prayed over her and when she left that night some of her symptoms had left her. When my friend brought her home, my friend's brother, the girl's father, apparently became angry saying something to the effect that we were giving her false hope and said something about wanting to sue us for this. This, I think is reflective of just how far away many Christians and certainly Catholic Christians are from understanding much of anything about God and His desire to heal us. In any case, my friend brought her back one more time. We prayed over her and when she went back to the doctor, the doctor said the disease was in remission. She was healed.

Another friend and her husband came over for prayers one night as she had been unable to carry a baby full term. Every pregnancy was ending in a miscarriage. The doctors told her she could no longer carry a baby full term. While praying over her for healing of this condition, I sensed that she was dealing with a lot of fear. When I asked her if that was true, she confirmed it. We prayed again and this time I quietly told the spirit of fear to leave her. When they got home that evening, she called and asked if I had cast out any spirits because she was belching all the way home. She said, "That was something she almost never did." I told her I had cast out spirits and asked if she was okay with that. She said she was okay as she knew a little bit about it. To make a long story short she and her husband had two more children after that and she never had another miscarriage. We all went to the same church and so we had the privilege of watching the two children grow up. Thanks Be to God for his great love for us.

We recently were asked by a friend to come to the hospital to pray over her husband who had just had a shoulder replacement and was in a lot of pain. It was the night before we were to leave for a two week Mediterranean cruise but we went to the hospital anyway. His wife and daughter were also there when we got there. We talked a while and then we all laid hands and prayed for the pain to cease and for a fast recovery. I happened to also pray that any and all illness present would leave. As we were walking down the hall his wife told us he had been diagnosed with Sundowners Syndrome, an early form of Alzheimer's, as I understand it. During the cruise, I prayed for both of them every day and the first Sunday we were back, I saw her at church and asked her when I could come over to pray for him. She asked, "What did I want to pray for?" When I told her the Sundowners Syndrome she told me the symptoms left him the night we prayed for his shoulder and had not returned. His doctor had confirmed that it was gone. Praise God!

Here is one other healing which had nothing to do with our praying but rather, with our daughters praying for her son. Our third daughter, Cathy, and her husband have three children. When their oldest, a boy, was in 8th grade, he was suffering from a painful back. Riley is very athletic and very disciplined to do exercises every day. He was being attended to by both a chiropractor and an orthopedic surgeon. One night Cathy said she was awakened by the Holy Spirit and was told to go and pray for her son. She said that since it was the middle of the night she went back to sleep. A few minutes later she was awakened again with the same message and again she went back to sleep. When she was awakened the third time she got the message and went into Riley's room and prayed over him. The next morning she was going to tell her husband what had happened but decided not to do so. When Riley came in for breakfast she also decided not to tell him. That afternoon they had a scheduled appointment with the chiropractor. So she picked Riley up from school and they went to the chiropractor who took one look at Riley and said "I don't know what has happened, but his back is in perfect alignment." She told Riley on the way out the door about praying over him the night before and his response was that he had awakened that morning pain free but did not say anything because he thought she might think he was just trying to skip the office visit. When the other doctor examined him a few days later, he agreed that Riley was healed. That speaks so much for only certain people having special gifts or for being "called" to the healing ministry. We'll talk about that later.

Chapter 16

How God Sees Us

I believe one of our biggest problems is seeing ourselves in our own minds and failing to see ourselves as God sees us. We take our experiences in life and we think that life defines who we really are. This view is a product of many things, such as seeing our failures throughout life. Even with this we take the world's view of success and we measure ourselves by it. This causes us to come up short. Many of us have been told in one way or another that we will never amount to anything. Many of the churches emphasize our sinfulness, and so we become sin conscious. One of the ways I saw myself was not only because I did not have a lot of self discipline, but that I saw others as having much more self discipline than I had. I really think it is one of the reasons I did not go to church for years. In my mind I could never live up to the standard that they set for themselves. I often told myself that if I had the self discipline of so and so I would rise to be the president of the company, any company. I also measured myself by how much money I had and, of course, I only compared myself with those who had more than I did. I am not talking about celebrities and famous people. I would compare myself to people I knew. I always saw myself as less. It is hard to love yourself when you take this kind of view of yourself. Throughout the New Testament we are told that we have been reconciled to God through the death and resurrection of Jesus, that we are God's children. We are told that He loves us far beyond what we can imagine. It is not just in the New Testament, but it is in the Old Testament as well. Let's look at just a couple of Scriptures so we can start to see how God views us.

Let's begin with the book of Psalms, Chapter 139.

> [13]For thou didst form my inward parts, thou didst knit me together in my mother's womb. [14]I praise thee, for thou art fearful and wonderful. Wonderful are thy works! Thou knows me right well; [15]my frame was not hidden from thee, when I was being made in secret, intricately wrought in the depths of the earth. [16]Thy eyes beheld my unformed substance; in thy book were written, every one of them, the days that were formed for me, when as yet there was none of them. [17]How precious to me are thy thoughts, O God! How vast is the sum of them! [18]If I would count them, they are more than the sand. When I awake, I am still with thee.

Here, God's Word tells us that He formed us, that His work is wonderful (that is you and I are wonderful), He knew exactly what He was doing, we are written in His book, His thoughts toward us are precious (that is how He sees us) and His precious thoughts toward us are endless. Wow! When I begin to believe this instead of what I have experienced in my life, all my negative thoughts just seem to melt away.

Let's go to the New Testament and look at 1 Timothy Chapter 4, verse 4.

> For everything created by God is good, and nothing is to be rejected if it is received with thanksgiving.

God created you and you are good, so stop rejecting this and start to revel in it. We need to be thankful for our creation which is part of his plan.

Let's look in Ephesians Chapter 1, beginning with verse 3.

> [3] Blessed be the God and Father of our Lord Jesus Christ, who has blessed us in Christ with every spiritual blessing in the heavenly places, [4] even as he chose us in him before the foundation of the world, that we should be holy and blameless before him. [5] He destined us in love to be his sons through Jesus Christ, according to the purpose of his will, [6] to the praise of his glorious grace which he freely bestowed on us in the Beloved. [7] In him we have redemption through his blood, the forgiveness of our trespasses, according to the riches of his grace [8] which he lavished upon us. [9] For he has made known to us in all wisdom and insight the mystery of his will, according to his purpose which he set forth in Christ [10] as a plan for the fullness of time, to unite all things in him, things in heaven and things on earth.

Wow! God has given us every spiritual blessing. He chose us in Him before the world began (that is truly mind blowing). He destines us in love to be his children through Christ and this is part of His will (God desires to do this. This can get overwhelming when you think about it). We actually should stop thinking about it but rather believe it and in believing, appropriate it into our lives. It goes on to tell us we have been redeemed through the blood of His son Jesus, and we have forgiveness of our mistakes according to the riches of his grace, which he freely gives to us. His plan is that we be united to him, and note it says both in heaven *and* on earth. This means we don't have to wait until we get to heaven to be united with God. It is a now thing.

Let's look at one more Scripture from Ephesians. Let's look in chapter 3 verses 14 through 20.

¹⁴ For this reason I bow my knees before the Father, ¹⁵ from whom every family in heaven and on earth is named, ¹⁶ that according to the riches of his glory he may grant you to be strengthened with might through his Spirit in the inner man, ¹⁷ and that Christ may dwell in your hearts through faith; that you, being rooted and grounded in love, ¹⁸ may have power to comprehend with all the saints what is the breadth and length and height and depth, ¹⁹ and to know the love of Christ which surpasses knowledge, that you may be filled with all the fullness of God. ²⁰ Now to him who by the power at work within us is able to do far more abundantly than all that we ask or think, ²¹ to him be glory in the church and in Christ Jesus to all generations, forever and ever. Amen.

The above tells us that we are strengthened by his Spirit deep inside us. But this all happens through faith in his word. We have a choice: have faith in what God tells us about us, or have faith in what life and the world and its ways tell us about us. The Word tells us we are grounded in love (Christ's love) so we may have the power to comprehend with all the saints (this includes you and me; we are saints in God's eye) and that when we believe this, we will know the overwhelming amount of God's love for us to the point where we will be filled with all the fullness of God. This all happens right here on earth!

In past chapters I shared with you some of our experiences with regard to healing, both physical healing and inner healing. For me, on a personal level, getting free from my emotional and spiritual pain via inner healing took a lot of work and it occurred over a long period of time. I want to tell you there is perhaps **a better way**. In the 8ᵗʰ chapter of the Gospel of John, Jesus states the following:

[31] Jesus then said to the Jews who had believed in him, "If you continue in my word, you are truly my disciples, [32] and you will know the truth, and the truth will make you free."

The act of continuing in God's word means to not only believe it but to live it. Believing is not an intellectual exercise. Faith, or believing, is an action. In the book of James it is stated very simply.

[17] So faith by itself, if it has no works, is dead.

So Jesus is telling us in the Gospel of John that continuing in his Word, the Word of God, means living it in one's life. He then says you will know the truth and the truth will set you free. Let me give you an example.

A number of years ago I was talking with a nun from our parish after Mass one Saturday morning. I was talking about the parable of the sower as described in Matthew 13.

That same day Jesus went out of the house and sat beside the sea. [2] And great crowds gathered about him, so that he got into a boat and sat there; and the whole crowd stood on the beach. [3] And he told them many things in parables, saying:

A man went out to sow. [4] And as he sowed, some seeds fell along the path, and the birds came and devoured them. [5] Other seeds fell on rocky ground, where they had not much soil, and immediately they sprang up, since they had no depth of soil, [6] but when the sun rose they were scorched; and since they had no root they withered away. [7] Other seeds fell upon thorns, and the thorns grew up and choked them. [8] Other seeds fell on good soil and brought forth grain, some a hundredfold, some sixty, some thirty. [9] He who has ears, let him hear.

I told her that I was fearful that I would somehow not make it in my walk with God. I was fearful that perhaps I did not have the required depth and it would all go away.

This nun surprised me when she quoted Philippians 1: 6.

> "And I am sure that he who began a good work in you will bring it to completion at the day of Jesus Christ."

When she quoted these words they just seemed to sink into my heart, and I knew from that moment on I no longer have to worry about, nor strive to be good enough to earn God's love. I was set free from the lie of believing that I have to earn God's love.

More recently in my life I have accepted the fact that I am an adopted son of God. I have accepted that as a son, I have open access to the Father, and that as a son; I am an heir to God's kingdom.

In Galatians chapter 4 the word of God tells us:

> [4] But when the time had fully come, God sent forth his Son, born of woman, born under the law, [5] to redeem those who were under the law, so that we might receive adoption as sons. [6] And because you are sons, God has sent the Spirit of his Son into our hearts, crying, "Abba! Father!" [7] So through God you are no longer a slave but a son, and if a son then an heir.

I found as I internalized this truth, that God sees me as his son. Then I found that I can love myself with all my warts and shortcomings. I am set free from the lie that I have to be someone or something other than who I am to be accepted and loved by God. Well, if God loves me as I am, because He sees me through the blood that was shed by Jesus, then I can certainly accept and love me as I am. As I do this, I am set free by virtue of the truth that I am a son of God

A friend of mine asked my wife and me to come over to his house to view some DVDs from a conference he and his wife had attended. The conference was called "Power and Love." They actually asked if we would like to view the DVDs for four Saturdays, as the conference they attended ran for four days. We reluctantly agreed to attend the first day only and would take a "wait and see attitude." After all, we are busy people, and four days was asking a lot from us. By the time the first talk was over, I knew I would be attending all four Saturdays, and my wife agreed. I can only that say watching the DVDs resulted in a life changing experience for me. The general theme of the conference, if I were to categorize it, was "coming to know who we are in Christ". When we know who we are in Christ we can more effectively to take the message of love to others.

In one of the early talks of the conference, the speaker quoted the following Scripture. I had heard this scripture many times before, only this time it just seemed to speak to me in a very deep and personal way. The Scripture is from Matthew Chapter 6.

> [33] But seek first his kingdom and his righteousness, and all these things shall be yours as well.

The first thing I did, without telling anyone, was to stop playing the lotto. Deep down I realized playing the lotto reflected my desire to have wealth and I knew I needed to have God first. An amazing thing happened immediately. A low level form of depression, which I was not even aware of, left me. The way I recognized this low level of depression was that I became more joy filled when I stopped playing the lotto.

Over the next few weeks I asked God to show me how to seek His kingdom. I told nobody about what I was asking God. In a sense I was almost embarrassed that I did not know how to seek His kingdom. Well, this same friend just happened to send me a YouTube link to an interview with the missionary evangelist, Heidi Baker on the CBN network. As I watched this interview two things happened to me. I saw Heidi Baker as another Mother Teresa. Or another way to put it is that I was immediately confronted with the fact that I was listening to a Holy Woman of God. In the interview she mentioned she had written a book called "Compelled by Love." I was moved to order the book. When I got it I realized the book was about the Beatitudes, which of course, answers the question about seeking the kingdom of God. I could not put the book down, and have read it several times because it touched me so deeply.

I was so moved by the book that I began to view some of the teachings she has done that are available on YouTube. I have been deeply touched by more than a few of the teachings, but I am compelled to mention one of them. She did a talk entitled "What Will You Do with Your Little Lunch?" In the talk she points out that when Jesus and His disciples were confronted with feeding the multitudes, the only food available was from a little boy who had a few fish and a few loaves of bread. The boy offered his little lunch and God multiplied what the boy had offered. I realized that all I had to do was offer what little love I had to others, and God would turn that love into whatever was needed.

The same day we were watching the DVDs on Power and Love, I saw in the spirit that a friend of ours was slowly having the life choked out of her by the Evil One via the many infirmities she had. I knew we needed to lay hands on her and pray against these illnesses. By strange coincidence she and her husband called that evening and asked if we wanted to meet for breakfast after church the next day. They agreed to come to the earlier service in order to meet us. While we were having breakfast I told her what I had seen in the spirit the day before. She confirmed it by nodding and weeping indicating that she felt that her life was slowly being taken from her. Anita and I reached over the table and prayed for her telling the infirmities to leave her body. Later in the week my wife called her and she said she was feeling much better.

I would be remiss if I did not share two other powerful things that happened to me regarding knowing the truth and the truth setting one free. I am in my seventies and I am not really sure we have enough money for retirement. The company where I had worked for over 30 years had sold our part of the business to another company that is headquartered outside of the USA. In any case, when in my early 50s, this new company froze our pension, telling us that whatever we were entitled to pension-wise at this point was all we would ever receive. They did set up a 401K for us to contribute to, and it appeared as if the market just seemed to drop in the areas I had my investments. I went to another company and the same thing seemed to happen there as well. Two years ago my boss called me into his office to tell me that my job would be ending a couple of years later. I joked with him asking if that meant I could plan my retirement cruise. He laughed and said yes I should plan on it. About a month later, I was praying and I asked God to give me a word for my problem. Now I must say I did not know what my problem was. I just knew I was feeling a bit down. Within seconds I heard Psalm 23 in my spirit.

I have a little history with the 23rd Psalm. When I was a young boy I remember our pastor telling us if we were to memorize any Scripture he suggested we start with the 23rd Psalm. Well I am not, nor was I ever, much of a memorizer. I told my wife I was going to memorize it and proceeded to do so. A couple of weeks later I got an e-mail telling about a Sunday school teacher who asked her class to memorize the 23rd Psalm. One of the boys in the class did not like to memorize. Boy, could I relate to that. So when he was called upon to recite the Psalm he stood up and said "The Lord is my Shepherd there is nothing I shall want…and no more needs to be said about it." Wow did that hit home. I stopped worrying about my retirement.

Once, I was at a tent meeting where Todd White spoke. I went up to him after one of his talks and thanked him for touching my life so deeply. I then said to him that sometimes it is hard to unlearn what we had been taught, such as, having to earn God's love. When I told Todd some things were hard to unlearn he expressed a sense of frustration. He said "I hear that over and over again." He told me to live the truth as I learned it, and in living it, that truth will set me free from the misconceptions and lies I had previously learned. In other words I don't have to unlearn, I only have to live in the truth and it will set me free.

The last thing I want to share has to do with being a child of God. Dan Mohler gave a teaching which I viewed on *You Tube* one day. The teaching revolves around the Scripture from Matthew Chapter 23.

⁹ And call no man your father on earth, for you have one Father, who is in heaven.

It caught my attention because some Christian denominations have a problem with Catholics calling their priests "father". This teaching has nothing to do with that, and I don't intend to go there. Basically what this teaching boils down to is that our Father in heaven is who we "come forth from." Psalm 139 tells us he knit us in our mother's womb. He created us. In Ephesians 1 it also says that God knew us before the world began. He just happened to use my mother and my father to be the instruments of my creation. While listening to this truth, I became totally free from all that I ever thought about regarding the imperfections of my parents, and also regarding my own imperfections. I am truly God's creation, and He created me to be His adopted son right now. I am living like a son and I can no longer remember any emotional pain, for example, related to the lack of affection that my mother had for me. The pain from that is no longer a part of my being.

When I was reviewing the contents of this book, and I got to the story of my anger toward my mother, I realized I no longer experienced any of the pain I had lived with for years. The change was so dramatic that I was tempted to remove the story from the book because now it is like it never happened. This is truly being set free by God's Word.

Chapter 17
God's Will is to Heal

Let's revisit the whole subject of healing, specifically, "Is it God's will to heal and if so why do some people not get healed?" Let's look at some Scripture passages on this subject. Psalm 103 verse 3 states that He forgives all our iniquities and heals all our diseases. It does not get much clearer than that. There is no disease He cannot nor will not heal.

The church teaches there is no sickness in heaven. So let's agree there is no sickness in heaven.

In Matthew 6, Jesus, teaches about prayer, among other things. In fact, that is where the Lord's Prayer comes from. In the 10th verse He says:

> 10 Thy kingdom come. Thy will be done, on earth as it is in heaven.

So Jesus tells us that God's will is to be done on earth just as it is in heaven. This would indicate to me that God wants healing to be done on earth.

In the Matthew Chapter 10 Jesus is talking to the twelve apostles and He says the following:

> 7 and preach as you go, saying, "The kingdom of heaven is at hand." 8 Heal the sick, raise the dead, cleanse the lepers, cast out demons. You received without paying, give without pay.

Notice Jesus tells us to heal the sick. Some will argue that he was only talking to the apostles. That is true, but we are called to share in the work of the apostles. In fact in the Catholic Church, Vatican II clearly states that all are to share in the apostolic works, so healing would be included. Read on.

In Luke chapter 10, Jesus is talking to the seventy, which means He is talking to other than the apostles. Here is what is said.

> [8] Whenever you enter a town and they receive you, eat what is set before you; [9] heal the sick in it and say to them, "The kingdom of God has come near to you."

I love this particular scripture for two reasons. He not only tells us to heal the sick but He tells us to do this wherever we are. He also tells us to heal the sick and then tell them about the Gospel.

My wife and I got into the practice of healing the sick when our daughter was attacked. (See chapter 1 of this book.) That was in 1980. We go to church every week and sometimes during the week. The first time I can remember hearing this scripture preached was when we listened to some DVDs on Power and Love in 2011. I began to question whether or not our church ever referenced this Scripture in its list of Sunday readings. I know that the Catholic Church has three Liturgical years defined with prescribed Scriptures to be read at each Mass during the liturgical year. I was so convinced it had never been read that as part of my research I went through the list of readings for the three liturgical years and I found out I was wrong. It is included on one of the Sundays in Year C. However I must add that I don't ever remember anyone preaching on this specific aspect of the reading. I am not saying it hasn't been preached while I was in attendance, I just don't remember it. "Where am I going with this?" one might ask. Let me make my case.

In the Gospel of Mark in the 16th chapter the following is said:

> 15 And he said to them, "Go into all the world and preach the gospel to the whole creation. 16 He who believes and is baptized will be saved; but he who does not believe will be condemned. 17 And these signs will accompany those who believe: in my name they will cast out demons; they will speak in new tongues; 18 they will pick up serpents, and if they drink any deadly thing, it will not hurt them; they will lay their hands on the sick, and they will recover."

Here too, Jesus said to take the message to the whole world. Furthermore he says these signs will follow those who believe. They will cast out demons…and they will lay hands on the sick, and they will recover.

It sounds like healing to me. Furthermore, it seems to tie healing and perhaps the success of it to the believer. I am not talking about the person getting healed having to believe, but it seems to say that the person who is doing the laying on of hands is to be the believer.

Let me tie in a couple more Scriptures. In the book of Romans it says in chapter 10.

> 14 But how are men to call upon him in whom they have not believed? And how are they to believe in him of whom they have never heard? And how are they to hear without a preacher? 15 And how can men preach unless they are sent? As it is written, "How beautiful are the feet of those who preach good news!" 16 But they have not all obeyed the gospel; for Isaiah says, "Lord, who has believed

what he has heard from us?" ¹⁷ So faith comes from what is heard, and what is heard comes by the preaching of Christ.

I would like to focus on the 17ᵗʰ verse although there is a lot said b*efore that*. *Among other things*, the preacher is sent to preach the good news. In any case, verse 17 tells us that faith comes from hearing the Word that is preached.

The point I am trying to make is that over the past 30 plus years I have no recall of hearing the message to go and heal the sick in whatever town I am in. Now I must admit I may not have heard, as opposed to that message not having been preached. In any case the result is the same. My faith to go heal the sick has not been stirred in this area due, at least in part, to not hearing it preached. I wonder if this does not contribute to the fact that very little healing takes place in most families and in many churches.

At this point I think we need the scriptural definition of faith. Even in this book I have used the word faith to mean more than one thing. So let's see what faith is from the scriptural definition as this is the faith (to believe) we are talking about in order to heal.

In the book of Hebrews, chapter 11, verse 1 it says:

Now faith is the assurance of things hoped for, the conviction of things not seen.

Verse 6 tells us,

And without faith it is impossible to please him. For whoever would draw near to God must believe that he exists and that he rewards those who seek him.

I think four comments are in order. I never saw this

before but I recently heard a man preach on this very verse and he emphasized that faith is NOW. It is not a mental thing, but what we know NOW. When we are talking about faith, we are talking about faith in God and his word. We often place our faith in what we experience or see. Take note that in verse 1, above, faith pertains to things not seen. Once we see it we no longer need faith to obtain it. The word conviction means we believe with a depth that does not allow us to be shaken. When our heart is convicted, we stand on it as unshakable truth regardless of what we might experience. The third point is that God is not angry with us and he is not out to get us. He wants to bless us. So when the Word tells us that without faith we cannot please God, I believe it is telling us that God wants to give to us but we cannot receive if we don't believe. Let me try to create a simple example. If someone tells you to go somewhere or do something and he will give you a gift, there is a good chance one might say to one's self this is too good to be true. The result of this kind of thinking is to not do what was prescribed and therefore not receive what was promised. I believe this is why God is not pleased when we show little or no faith, for He cannot bless us as much as He desires.

Let me make one more point. In Hebrews chapter 4, the writer is talking about entering into God's rest. Verse 2 states the following:

> [2] For good news came to us just as to them; but the message which they heard did not benefit them, because it did not meet with faith in the hearers.

When we hear the word it only changes us when we hear it with faith which means we hear it and apply it to our lives.

I have had people from my church tell me it is just not a

practice in our faith to lay hands on the sick. Wow! That speaks volumes. I wonder if it ties directly to the point I was trying to make, above, that it is just not taught and therefore it might just limit our faith in this area of our walk. I do believe that had my wife and I not laid hands on our daughter she would most likely be a cripple today, some 30 years later. In fact had there not been a movement of the Holy Spirit in the churches I would never have read the books on healing that got us started down the path to healing.

We need to talk briefly about two other aspects of God's word which tie into healing. One is this notion of the Kingdom of God. The other is what role love plays in the equation. Let's look at a couple of Scriptures in these areas. I am sure there are more in addition to what we will be looking at.

Regarding the Kingdom of God, the Gospel of Matthew, in the 6th chapter tells us the following:

> [33] But seek first his kingdom and his righteousness, and all these things shall be yours as well.

In 1 Corinthians chapter 4, Saint Paul tells us about the kingdom of God:

> [20] For the kingdom of God does not consist in talk but in power.

So the power to heal lies in the kingdom of God. In 1 Corinthians chapter 2 Saint Paul tell us the following:

> [5] that your faith might not rest in the wisdom of men but in the power of God.

In The 5th chapter of Galatians Saint Paul states the following.

⁵ For through the Spirit, by faith, we wait for the hope of righteousness. ⁶ For in Christ Jesus neither circumcision nor un-circumcision is of any avail, but faith working through love.

The 6ᵗʰ verse tells us that the only thing that matters to Christ is faith working through love. So the key here is to have both faith and to live it out through love. This is where the power to heal takes place. I told you earlier in the book that God wanted me to learn to love myself. If I cannot love myself I don't have much in the tank to love others.

I just have to add in another scripture from the Gospel of John. Jesus tells us:

¹² "Truly, truly, I say to you, he who believes in me will also do the works that I do; and greater works than these will he do, because I go to the Father. ¹³ Whatever you ask in my name, I will do it, that the Father may be glorified in the Son 14 if you ask anything in my name, I will do it."

¹⁵ "If you love me, you will keep my commandments. ¹⁶ And I will pray the Father, and he will give you another Counselor, to be with you forever, ¹⁷ even the Spirit of truth, whom the world cannot receive, because it neither sees him nor knows him; you know him, for he dwells with you, and will be in you"

Wow! If we believe Jesus, and Jesus is the Word of God, then we will do the works he did and greater. There is a test of the depth of one's faith and one's ability to love. Those six verses sum up so much of what we have been talking about. There is even an extra thing or two added. In verses 13 and 14 He says, "Whatever you ask not only will He do it, but that it glorifies the Father." In verses 16 and 17 He tells us that He will pray and God will send his spirit to dwell in us. It is truly mind blowing.

So there is one more question I want to address regarding this faith thing. I have to admit I have laid hands on people, including in my own family who did not get healed. What do I do about that? If I can, time allowing, I continue to pray over them. I might pray with a person several times in a session like I did when I prayed over the woman who could not carry a baby full term. Did I know she was healed when she left? No, I did not. In that case I could not know whether or not she was healed until after she got pregnant again. I just relied on God's Word, Mark 16, quoted above. I told you earlier that we prayed over Linda during the healing retreat and then for several nights at home after the retreat before her back was healed. I was mentally prepared and determined to pray for as long as it took in this case, because I did not believe God wanted her to be crippled.

So the question becomes, what do I do when we pray and the person is not healed and circumstances do not allow continued prayer? I go to be alone with God in my own private prayer time and I ask for more faith and for more love. In fact, my basic prayer these days is to ask God for three things regarding love. I ask for a heart to love as Jesus loved, I ask for a heart that is pure in its intention, and I ask God to help me see people as He sees them. I also listen to preaching that addresses the area where my faith may be weak. Thank God for *YouTube*.

I think it is a human tendency to build our own theology around what we see in the world rather than believing God's word. Is that not what happened in the Garden of Eden? We, the human race, created our own kingdom and from that we set our own rules and a lot of those rules were based on our own experience. In effect, we place our kingdom (that which we experience) above God's kingdom and His word. Another way I like to state it is that when Jesus taught the Lord's Prayer He said "thy kingdom come", not "my kingdom come".

Chapter 18

Apart From Me
You Can Do Nothing

In the gospel of John, the 15th chapter Jesus tells us that he is the vine and we are the branches. Let's examine this:

> I am the true vine, and my Father is the vinedresser. [2] Every branch of mine that bears no fruit, he takes away, and every branch that does bear fruit he prunes, that it may bear more fruit. [3] You are already made clean by the word which I have spoken to you. [4] Abide in me, and I in you. As the branch cannot bear fruit by itself, unless it abides in the vine, neither can you, unless you abide in me. [5] I am the vine, you are the branches. He who abides in me, and I in him, he it is that bears much fruit, for apart from me you can do nothing. [6] If a man does not abide in me, he is cast forth as a branch and withers; and the branches are gathered, thrown into the fire and burned. [7] If you abide in me, and my words abide in you, ask whatever you will, and it shall be done for you. [8] By this my Father is glorified, that you bear much fruit, and so prove to be my disciples. [9] As the Father has loved me, so have I loved you; abide in my love. [10] If you keep my commandments, you will abide in my love, just as I have kept my Father's commandments and abide in his love. [11] These things I have spoken to you, that my joy may be in you, and that your joy may be full.

In the 5th verse Jesus tells us that apart from Him we can do nothing. I asked a man who I have known over the years to look at my book with the possibility of writing an endorsement. I have to add that every time I've been around him, I've felt the Holy Spirit was speaking directly through him to me. A recent visit was no exception. While my wife and I were visiting with him, he told us how years ago he had been seeking spiritual direction and the person he asked to be his spiritual director told him he would start in the Gospel of John. He told the director that he was familiar with the Gospel of John. I thought the very same thing as my friend spoke. The spiritual director then said he would begin with John 15, and I thought, "I am familiar with that. It's about the vine and the branches." The spiritual director then said he would zero in on verse 5, and, in particular, the last part of verse 5, "Apart from me you can do nothing." My friend went on to say he spent the next six years contemplating those words. Then it hit me that I did not really know what it meant, but I knew the Holy Spirit wanted me talk about it as part of this book. What does it mean to be apart from Jesus, but also what does it mean to be with Jesus? I believe it all hinges on dying to self. When we don't die to self we stand in the way of being close to Christ. On the other hand, when we die to self, we are with Jesus in that he takes over our lives. Dying to self is not a onetime act. We must die to self in every situation if we want the love and the power of Christ operating through us. So now I have to ask myself, "What does it mean to die to self?" For me, dying to self means to look at everything from Jesus' perspective...and being willing to act on that. In a large way that includes my judgments, my ego, my ambition, my prayer life, and my priorities. I try and measure all of these things from His perspective...not my own. I've found that when I see things from His perspective, things in my own life change. Then I am "abiding" in Him. When

I don't die to self, I remain number one…not Christ… and then I can do nothing. Let me give you an example of ego or pride. A lady asked to see my wife and me about her marriage situation. She came to see us without her husband. She was also of the Jewish faith. After we talked for a while we told her we really did not counsel as we did not think we were qualified to do counseling. We told her we prayed over people and God healed them. We asked her if that was okay. She said "Yes." Then we told her we prayed in the name of Jesus and asked if she could accept that. Again she said "Yes." Finally I told her that often times when I did not know what to pray for that we prayed in tongues. We told her that when we prayed in tongues it was actually the Holy Spirit praying for us, taken from Romans 8:26-27.

> Likewise the Spirit helps us in our weakness; for we do not know how to pray as we ought, but the Spirit himself intercedes for us with sighs too deep for words. [27] And he who searches the hearts of men knows what is the mind of the Spirit, because the Spirit intercedes for the saints according to the will of God.

She agreed to have us pray. When we finished we asked her if she experienced anything when we prayed and the only thing she said was that when I prayed, it sounded like Hebrew. I thought "Wow, I am praying in Hebrew." I asked if she knew what I said in Hebrew, but she did not. The lady left and the next few times we saw her she and her husband were walking around holding hands and looked like newlyweds. We have no idea what happened. We did not approach her as she had asked us not to tell her husband she had come to see us.

A few months later, a friend asked us if we would talk about the gifts of the Holy Spirit at a Life in the Spirit

Seminar he was coordinating. We said yes, and asked him to send us an outline of what he wanted us to talk about, as we wanted to be sure our talk fit in with the rest of the talks from the seminar. We did not understand parts of the outline he sent us, so I woke up at 2:00 A.M. two days before we were to give the talk, and I asked God to help me create an outline. When I finished I printed it out and went back to bed. The next morning, I told my wife we needed to go over the outline and decide who would talk about what. When we went over the outline, I had added a section on pride. My wife said, "You take that section." I prayed to ask God what we should talk about in each section. When I got to the one on pride, I asked God for an example in which I was prideful with regard to the gift of the Spirit. He called to mind the same incident above where the lady said my praying in tongues sounded like Hebrew. I asked God, "Where was the pride?" His response was, "I made it sound like Hebrew. You were not speaking in Hebrew."

Another example in which I had to die to self occurred a number of years ago when I would watch the Benny Hinn miracle crusades hoping to learn something about the technique or method used for getting results when praying for healing. One time, either on his TV show or in a book he had written, he stated that he spent something like three hours a day in prayer. My immediate reaction was that I could never do that. In fact, I told myself that I didn't know if I wanted to pay that steep a price. This kind of thinking pointed directly to self and an attitude of, "Don't mess up the life style I am living." Over time I came to realize that healing was not a method, but that it came from a relationship with Christ. Furthermore, if I were to have a closer relationship with Christ, at the very least I needed to spend time with him.

In spending more time with Him, I continually have to die to self to not watch the clock or to measure how fruitful my time with him went. Did I feel close or did I not feel close? If I heard a word directly from Him than I judged my time with Him was more fruitful than if I did not hear something directly from Him. That kind of thinking has to go, as it is centered on me and not on Him.

In the Gospel of Mark in the fifth chapter verse 30 it says:

> And Jesus, perceiving in himself that power had gone forth from him, immediately turned about in the crowd, and said, "Who touched my garments?"

Jesus perceived that power had gone out of Him. The kingdom of God is about power. So I can think of myself as a battery that has the potential to hold the power of Christ. In order for that power to be at its maximum I need to be charged just like a battery needs to be charged. The best way to bring a battery up to its full capacity is to use a trickle charger. A trickle charger takes time to get the battery to its full potential. That is what spending time with Christ does. It happens over a longer period of time and is not perceivably measurable along the way.

A while back, my wife and I were out of the country and facing a 12 to 13 hour flight. As it turned out we ended up seated next to a person who was having problems with her knee. When the plane was in the air we offered to pray over the knee and she accepted our invitation. After praying over her she started to tell a little bit about herself and her situation. About that time the movie came on and we all agreed to watch the movie. I could not get into the movie. For the next two hours or so, I spent my time lifting this person up to God in prayer. When the movie ended my wife excused herself to use the rest room. I turned to the lady and began to speak words of knowledge about her situation, about her past, and how it affected her relationships. While I was speaking she began to cry and nodded in agreement that everything I was saying was true. It was not as though God was telling me what to say. It was that God was using my tongue, lips, and vocal chords to tell her what He wanted to say. I was almost as overwhelmed by it as she was. The point I want to make is that spending that time in prayer seemed to release God's power to speak the words of knowledge she needed to hear in order to lead her toward healing her relationship with someone very close to her. I then offered to send her a draft of this book, which she accepted. I sent it to her via e-mail when I got home. She apparently read the draft I sent to her, and she told me how much it was helping her with her problem.

In the 7th verse He clarifies things a little further. He says if you abide in Him as well as have His words abide in us, then when you ask anything it shall be done for you. This is another example of what I was not seeing that before I started to write this book. That is, I never saw what verse 7 said to the point of taking His Word into my mind and my heart.

So the questions of what it means to abide in Christ and what it means to have His words abide in us must be asked.

When the Word abides in someone it is because they have been putting it into practice and it is almost second nature. When His Word abides in me, I find that it is automatic and something I don't even think about having into practice. For example, in the first chapter of James, it tells us that if we need wisdom, we should simply ask God and He will give it to us. I have been exercising that part of the Word for so long that I don't even think about it. I just do it. Another area of the Word that abides in me is in Psalm

103 verse 3 which says "He forgives all our iniquities and heals all of our diseases." So when I hear someone is sick, my automatic thought is that God will heal that person. Does it always happen that the person gets healed? No, but for me that just means I need to spend more time with Christ.

Recently I was on a retreat put on by Christians in Commerce. On Saturday afternoon after one of the talks there was time set aside in small groups for the group members to pray over each other. While they were praying over me, the person leading the prayer suggested I see myself walking in the park with Jesus. The moment he said that, I saw myself in the park on the basketball court dunking the ball with my right hand. I thought that is impossible. I am predominately a left hander. I could not even dunk the ball when I was a young man in the athletic prime of my life. On top of all that, I have bad knees now. When they finished praying over me I told them what I saw and said "I have no idea what that means." The following morning during my prayer time I asked the Lord what that meant, about my dunking the ball and doing it right handed. His response was "If you stay close to me, even what appears to be impossible will be a slam dunk."

So when someone asks, "Why doesn't God heal everyone?" perhaps the place to look for the answer is in one's relationship with Christ and His Word. I have seen many healed but not all that I have prayed for were healed. When I don't see healing, I ask, "How can I get closer, or how can I know Him better?" I never look at God and ask why wasn't this person healed? That kind of thinking tends to end in my pointing a finger at God. Rather, I have to look at my own relationship with Him, my knowledge of Him, and my understanding of who He is. It is then that I need to grow in that relationship via prayer and by reading His Word. I have to believe that God is always faithful to "charge my battery" if you will.

Chapter 19

The Healing Power of Tithing

I would be remiss if I did not talk about tithing and the healing influence it has on my wife and me. I was not going to include this subject in the book, but last night, as He often does, God spoke to me and encouraged me to include the subject of tithing. You might ask, what can tithing possibly do with healing? Let me see if I can develop that.

Let's start with a couple of Scriptures that relate to tithing. In the book of Haggai, chapter 2 verse 8 it says

> [8] The silver is mine, and the gold is mine, says the LORD of hosts.

It is my understanding that all money systems are based on silver and gold. One can assume then that all the money is God's money.

Now let's look at the book of Malachi chapter 3 versus 7 thru 12.

> [7] From the days of your fathers you have turned aside from my statutes and have not kept them. Return to me, and I will return to you, says the LORD of hosts. But you say, "How shall we return?" [8] Will man rob God? Yet you are robbing me. But you say, "How are we robbing thee?" In your tithes and offerings. [9] You are cursed with a curse, for you are robbing me; the whole nation of you. [10] Bring the full tithes into the storehouse, that there may be food in my house; and thereby

put me to the test, says the LORD of hosts, if I will not open the windows of heaven for you and pour down for you an overflowing blessing. [11] I will rebuke the devourer for you, so that it will not destroy the fruits of your soil; and your vine in the field shall not fail to bear, says the LORD of hosts. [12] Then all nations will call you blessed, for you will be a land of delight, says the LORD of hosts.

God calls us to return to Him by bringing in the full tithe. Return to Him means do things His way. In the 10th verse He tells us to test Him in this and to see if He will not pour out an overflow of blessings. I am told, and I don't know if there are other places in the Word of God, that this is the one place where God invites us to test Him. I wonder if He does that because He knows we have trouble parting with our money and our possessions. In any case there have been many times when I tried to witness to someone about tithing and I was told, "Don't try to tell me God has blessed you financially just because you tithe." Or they will ask, "How do you know you are being treated any differently than if you had not tithed?" In any case, I get the distinct impression that many people just don't believe God's Word in this area. I will also have to say that was exactly where I was before I finally trusted God's invitation and began to tithe. Deep inside, I was hoping to be able to retire early and enjoy the "good life" before I got too old. I just could not make sense out of giving more money away than what I was already giving.

In verse 11, God tells us that when we tithe, he will protect us from the devourer (evil one). Keep this in mind and I will tell you how that seemed to play out in our life. He also tells us in verse 9 that we are cursed for robbing Him by not bringing in the full tithe.

Since I have never heard a teaching on tithing at any of the churches I ever attended I found I had to seek the teaching on my own. My wife and I listened to some teachings regarding the subject of tithing but we could not convince ourselves to do so. I mean by this time we were in our late 50s and time was passing quickly. One weekend we attended a convention in the Los Angeles area hosted by the Catholic Charismatic Renewal. Throughout the weekend my wife and I both heard God calling us to two things. One was to send our son Christopher to Loyola Marymount University (LMU) and the other was to begin to tithe. Now I have to tell you this really did not make sense. We still had one daughter in college attending the University of Arizona. She had one year remaining. LMU is a Jesuit University and is considerably more expensive that the state universities in Arizona. Then there was this tithe thing (plus as I mentioned I was really hoping to retire early). During the weekend Anita told me she had experienced a healing when the speaker prayed for the attendees at the end of his/her talk. I was really excited to hear more details about what she experienced until she told me that the healing had to do with the death of her father while we were sophomores in college. The cause of her father's death appeared to be somewhat related to financial stress. She was afraid to press me in any way to be open to sending Christopher to LMU because of the possible stress. She said she was now free of that fear and wanted to talk more about sending him there. I really did not want to hear that because I really preferred not to spend the money.

At the closing Mass for the convention, the main speaker asked Fr John Hampsch to say a few words about financial giving prior to their asking for a free will offering. Father Hampsch spoke for what seemed to be an eternity, and appeared to cite every Scripture on tithing that existed in the Bible. We were tired merely from attending the conference all weekend, and I found his talk quite annoying. What I did not realize until sometime later was that the Holy Spirit was convicting me to commit to tithing and I just did not want to do so.

During this discernment I also tried to use the possibility of our three girls being upset because they had gone to the state university and now we would be sending Christopher to LMU. We decided to ask them and not only did they think it would be wonderful if we sent him there, but they offered to help any way they could. There went that excuse.

A few weeks later Anita and I were driving somewhere when she asked if I wanted to listen to a teaching tape we had in the car with us. I said sure and she asked "What about the teaching that addressed tithing?" My answer was "I did not want to listen to that particular subject unless she was ready to begin tithing." I was hoping she would pick a different tape. She did not select a different tape so in went the tape on tithing. By the time we got to our destination we were convicted to begin tithing. I told Anita I would like to have our pastor listen to the tape. Her answer was "Just how do you expect to pull that off?" I dropped the subject. We sat down to work out a budget to tithe, and I realized I could not do so and send Christopher to LMU at the same time. So I told God we would tithe but the tuition to LMU had to be considered as part of the tithe. I got the sense that was OK with God.

The first thing that happened occurred a month or two later. I was at work when our pastor called me and told me that he had just come from an advisory board meeting. Our names had been suggested to speak the following week at every Mass on the subject of Sacrificial Giving (the annual collection request.) We had told no one we had started tithing. We just started giving more to the church and to other areas. I asked our pastor if we had been suggested to speak because we had started to tithe. His response was that he did not know we were tithing and then he asked me, "What prompted you to tithe?" I told him about the tape we had listened to, and immediately he became interested, asking if he could get a copy of it for himself. When I told Anita what had transpired she said, "You are amazing." I said, "No, our God is amazing."

When we talked at all the Masses, we chose to talk about our decision to tithe. We basically stated that the world's ways did not seem to work, and that we had decided to try God's way, especially in light of verse 10 above, with God inviting us to try Him in this. We received a standing ovation at several of the Masses and had a fair sized number of people tell us they were going to look into tithing

About the same time frame, a friend, who was also an assistant principal at the local Jesuit High School, Brophy Prep, had invited Anita to look into leaving the public schools and teach at his school where they were looking to hire a Spanish teacher. When she interviewed they told her they could not match what she was making but would like to make an offer anyway. Incidentally, the retirement plan was not nearly as good as the public school plan either. We truly believed God was calling Anita to make the change so we decided to pray to come up with a salary figure we could live with. We both heard the same number, and coincidently that was exactly what they offered. Anita took the job.

So there we were, not only sending our son to a private university, but we were entering into tithing, and Anita was taking a reduced salary along with a reduced retirement potential.

When the first semester ended, it was time to pay the tuition for both Cathy and Christopher. That depleted our entire savings. On top of that we were not earning enough money between both our salaries such that we would be able to save enough money to pay Christopher's tuition the following August. Thank God Cathy was graduating so we would have no more expenses there.

A week or so before the next semester was to begin, the phone rang and Anita answered spending the next few minutes speaking Spanish. When she got off the phone she told me the call was from the mother of two boys from Mexico who were attending classes at her high school to learn English. She had both boys in one of her classes. The mother was requesting of us to consider taking them in to live with us, because the family with whom they were living had many children, and it was a bit hectic for them to study. Anita went on to tell the mother she would get back to her after she had discussed with me the possibility of our housing the two boys. We prayed about it and we concluded we had the room and would just stretch our food budget to house the boys. When their mother called back a couple of days later, Anita told her we would be happy to house her boys. The mother surprised Anita by asking if $400.00 a month would be enough. She said that would be fine, as we were going to house them for nothing. A few days later the mother and father, a daughter and the two boys arrived. The daughter was apparently along to help her parents with the 12 hour drive from their house in Mexico to ours. The first thing that happened was that we just seem to bond with the entire family despite the fact the parents did not speak English and I did not speak Spanish. The boy's mother took Anita aside and asked if she could just pay $300.00 a month as the original amount seemed high. Since we were going to house the boys for nothing Anita said of course it would be fine. The mother then handed Anita $600.00 for the first month. She had meant $300.00 per boy. During the semester we were truly blessed having the boys living with us. We not only were blessed, but we bonded with the boys as if they were our own. When the older boy graduated, the family came up from Mexico and we all celebrated the occasion at a nice restaurant. Afterward, they packed up to leave. As they were ready to drive away, the older boy handed us an envelope and asked us not to open it until they had left. As they drove off we opened the envelope and inside there was a letter in which he told us that because he had come to live with us he now knew that God loved him. We were truly blessed.

That summer they called and asked if one of their cousins could come live with us while he also attended Brophy with the younger brother. During that year, we started to get phone calls from Mexican families from as far away as Mexico City, asking if their boys could live with us when they came to the US to learn English. I will have to say the greedy side of me surfaced as I saw the possibility of extra income for years to come. It never happened. By the time the second school year of housing the boys ended I had received both raises and bonuses at work and the need for extra income to pay for Christopher's tuition at LMU was no longer there. To make a long story short, sending Christopher to LMU was easier financially then sending the others to the state university.

As Christopher was entering his senior year, our daughter Cathy became engaged and had plans for a wedding the following spring. She asked if we could provide a wedding reception at one of the nice hotels. I thought "Here we go again. How are we going to pay for this?" Guess what? The phone rang and it was a family from the same city in Mexico asking if we could house their son while he lived here improving his English. That extra money helped pay for the wedding, especially since he almost never ate with us and only used our house to sleep and to shower before he left each day. He actually attended classes at ASU, and he took flying lessons at a flying school. A week or so before the wedding day, Carlos said he had truly appreciated living with us and that his father wanted to thank us by hosting us and another couple in their villa in Mazatlan, Mexico. Their condo was on the golf course there. When we and our friends got to the condo, they had a servant to take care of whatever we needed. They provided us with a surrey to drive around town and all the golf we wanted to play was paid for by the boy's father. Does God pour out blessing or does He not?

I just shared the financial blessings we received when we first started to tithe. There were many other blessings as well. It is just easier to describe quantifiable blessing such as what I described. Tithing is not a matter of giving more money so that God will multiply the "investment." It is not like telling you spouse what you would like for your birthday, and then having the gift you asked for show up wrapped in a box.

Tithing is God's way of asking you to *trust* Him.

So where is the healing power associated with tithing? Let me tell you what happened to us. First I like to joke and say our pocket book was healed. From the time we started tithing it seems like we were never in a state of want or stress financially. This does not mean we just keep spending expecting God to cover the tab. Until we started tithing the area of finances was perhaps the area where we, as a married couple, experienced the most bickering. We each tended to question how the other person wanted to spend our money. While this did not happen all the time, it did occur far too often. I can honestly state this type of bickering just went away when we started tithing without our trying to make it go away. When I noticed the part about protection from the evil one and the curse, mentioned above, I wondered if we were not dealing in the spiritual world when we were bickering. I had to ask myself, were we being harassed, if you will, by the evil one to fight about how we looked at our finances? I cannot come up with any other explanation, especially in light of the fact that we did nothing consciously to stop the bickering.

When we continued to tithe, I realized I was no longer worried about having enough money for retirement. My desire to retire early left me, and I ended up actually working past the normal retirement age, and truly enjoyed what I was doing. That one thing in itself had a healing effect. The stress was gone in this area of my life. Every so often I tended to wonder why we decided to have Anita leave the public school system where her retirement would have been considerably higher. When that kind of thinking crept in, I simply recalled how God called us to make that change, and relied on the fact that He would provide whatever we needed.

One evening, Anita and I were getting ready to talk to a group of people at our church on the subject of forgiveness. We were in the school library. A homeless man came into the room and walked up to me asking if I could give him some money for a bus ticket to Los Angeles. The man obviously had not bathed in days or perhaps weeks and he had a strong presence of alcohol on his breath. I told him if he would wait for us to make our presentation I would take him to the bus station and buy his ticket. In my mind the bus station was a number of miles away so I wondered if he was just trying to hustle me. I don't know why, but I asked him how much he needed for the bust ticket. He said he needed $43.00. I looked in my wallet and I had two twenty dollar bills and three singles. I gave him the $43.00. A couple of things happened: He rushed out of the library a happy man. My wife said, "What did you just do?" I told her what happened and she just shrugged her shoulders and walked over to the podium where were to speak. Notice, there was no bickering. Despite the fact that I wondered if the man had conned me out of $43.00 I became filled with unspeakable joy. Over the years, I sometimes wondered about what had happened there, especially in light of how far away I thought the bus station was. When I was writing this chapter and the memory of this came back to include it in the chapter, the Holy Spirit reminded me that there was a Greyhound bus stop about ½ mile from our church. I will never be able to answer the question as to why he walked up to me and asked for $43.00.

In the Gospel of Luke, chapter 6 verse 38 it says:

> [38] give, and it will be given to you; good measure, pressed down, shaken together, running over, will be put into your lap. For the measure you give will be the measure you get back.

Let's look at the book of Dueteronomy in chapter 30 versus 15-19.

> [15] See, I have set before you this day life and good, death and evil. [16] If you obey the commandments of the LORD your God which I command you this day, by loving the LORD your God, by walking in his ways, and by keeping his commandments and his statutes and his ordinances, then you shall live and multiply, and the LORD your God will bless you in the land which you are entering to take possession of it. [17] But if your heart turns away, and

you will not hear, but are drawn away to worship other gods and serve those, [18] I declare to you this day, that you shall perish; you shall not live long in the land which you are going over the Jordan to enter and possess. [19] I call heaven and earth to witness against you this day, that I have set before you life and death, blessing and curse; therefore choose life, that you and your descendants may live.

In verse 19 the word tells us He gives us a choice: we can choose life or death, the blessing or the curse.

Remember in Malachi chapter 3, verse 9 the word says we are living under the curse by not bringing in the full tithe. He also says *trust* me by bringing in the tithe. I wonder then if we are choosing the curse by not tithing and are we choosing the blessing (life) by choosing to tithe. It appears this way to me.

I think *trust* is the most important point in our relationship with God. I believe that in order to have a true relationship with someone we have to be able to *trust* the other person. Choosing to tithe is answering the invitation to *trust* God. I found that our relationship was greatly heightened when we decided to *trust* God and tithe. This was healing for our relationship.

Chapter 20

Being Born Again

Prior to wrapping this book up, I want to address the subject of "Being Born Again." Because I am not a theological expert on this subject, I will stick to my observations and my personal experience of being born again.

Before telling of my own experience, let me say a few words from what I learned about the Catholic teaching on the subject. Much to my surprise I found the following in the Catechism of the Catholic Church. I was surprised because the subject is seldom talked about from the pulpit, and when it is brought up, it has always sounded to me like the priest was trying to play down the subject (in light of what is being said in some other churches about having to be born again to be saved.) I can honestly say I do not remember times when the subject was talked about in any great depth. That being said, here is a quote from the Catechism.

> 526) To become a child in relation to God is the condition for entering the kingdom. [205] For this, we must humble ourselves and become little. Even more: to become "children of God" we must be "born from above" or "born of God". [206] Only when Christ is formed in us will the mystery of Christmas be fulfilled in us. [207] Christmas is the mystery of this "marvelous exchange":

In the Gospel of John, chapter 3 it says the following:

[1] Now there was a man of the Pharisees, named Nicodemus, a ruler of the Jews. [2] This man came

to Jesus by night and said to him, "Rabbi, we know that you are a teacher come from God; for no one can do these signs that you do, unless God is with him." ³ Jesus answered him, *"Truly, truly, I say to you, unless one is born anew, he cannot see the kingdom of God."* ⁴ Nicodemus said to him, "How can a man be born when he is old? Can he enter a second time into his mother's womb and be born?" ⁵ Jesus answered, *"Truly, truly, I say to you, unless one is born of water and the Spirit, he cannot enter the kingdom of God. ⁶ That which is born of the flesh is flesh, and that which is born of the Spirit is spirit. ⁷ Do not marvel that I said to you, 'You must be born anew.'"*

So it is clear that Jesus said one must be born again and the Catholic Church's teaching says the same thing. The argument then becomes, "When is one born again?" Some say it is at baptism, while others say when one receives the Sacrament of Confirmation, still others say it comes when you pray the prayer accepting Jesus as your personal savior. It sure does get confusing to me.

Let's try to look at it from another angle. In both the Gospel and in the Catechism of the Catholic Church cited above, there is a direct connection between being born again (being born from above) and the Kingdom of God. It has been my observation that for many Christians the Kingdom of God means going to heaven. When this is the case, Christianity becomes a kind of insurance policy to get into heaven when one dies.

The Scriptures tell us in 1 Corinthians chapter 4:

> ²⁰ For the kingdom of God does not consist in talk but in power.

In chapter 17, above, we talked about God's will is to heal.

In both Matthew 10 and Luke 10, this is spelled out.

I know I do not have the power to heal anyone. That power comes from God. The ability to heal came to me when I was "baptized" in the Holy Spirit. In fact I have discovered in my own life that being "born again" also produced in me a much greater ability to love than I ever experienced before.

So maybe the questions that should be asked are: "When you were baptized, or when you received Confirmation, or when you prayed the prayer to accept Jesus as your Lord and savior, did you step into the power of God? And how did that power manifest itself in your life? Did you begin laying hands on people and they got healed?"

In John 14:15-17 Jesus says:

> [15] "If you love me, you will keep my commandments. [16] And I will pray the Father, and he will give you another Counselor, to be with you for ever, [17] even the Spirit of truth, whom the world cannot receive, because it neither sees him nor knows him; you know him, for he dwells with you, and will be in you."

Then it seems to me we must heal the sick in whatever city we are in (Luke 10), because that is what Jesus commanded.

The Catechism cited above, points out that we must become little, or humble, for this to happen. This is in line with the gospel which says in Matthew, chapter 18:

> At that time the disciples came to Jesus, saying, "Who is the greatest in the kingdom of heaven?" [2] And calling to him a child, he put him in the midst of them, [3] and said, *"Truly, I say to you, unless you turn and become like children, you will never enter the*

kingdom of heaven. [4] *Whoever humbles himself like this child, he is the greatest in the kingdom of heaven"*

When one become like a little child one becomes dependent upon one's parent, which is exactly what we must do if we want to operate in the Kingdom of God. I have found that when I pray over someone and I enter into that prayer thinking I know what the person needs, nothing seems to happen. On the other hand when I can yield to Christ, then something happens much more frequently. So my battle, if you will, is to try to empty myself of my thoughts and I try to yield to Him.

Let me share with you a synopsis of my journey to become born again. In the Catholic Church the baptism of the Holy Spirit was resurrected in the 1960's. This movement in the Catholic Church was given the title of the Charismatic Renewal. This renewal spread rapidly through parts of the Catholic Church. I say parts of the church, because not everyone in the church participated in this renewal. Around the same time, two other renewals were taking place. One was called the Cursillo and the other the Marriage Encounter. My wife and I had attended the Marriage Encounter in 1976 and had a life changing conversion, as I described earlier in the book.

In 1980 when I had my nervous breakdown I began to seek healing. A lady who owned a religious bookstore which I frequented told me one day about a "Life in The Spirit" seminar that was about to take place at a local parish. The Life in the Spirit seminar was the main teaching vehicle utilized by the Charismatic Renewal to prepare people for the baptism of the Holy Spirit. I was not really interested in attending the seminar, mainly because I judged I was already walking with God. What more did I need? She then mentioned that as part of the seminar they were going to set one evening aside just for "healing of memories" (healing). That got my attention. So we went to the seminar.

I went with a bit of an attitude. After all, I had already found God, so my attendance was not with my heart open to anything new. During the seminar they had teachings on different aspects of life in the Holy Spirit that included Scripture references and small sharing groups. Each small group had a group leader. They also sent us home with Scriptures to read and to study. I did very little of that. In fact, one evening our group leader called to see how we were doing with the Scripture reading and I basically told her I did not have time to do the reading. In the last session of the seminar, teams of people prayed over each of us for the baptism of the Holy Spirit. In my case, nothing seemed to happen. I experienced nothing and I certainly did not appear to receive any of the New Testament spiritual gifts. It would be an understatement to say I wasn't very open to anything outside my own little kingdom.

About a year after we began presenting our healing workshops, we were invited to give a workshop for the Charismatic Renewal prayer group leaders. During that workshop, during the foot washing experience, the lady that had been our group leader in the Life in the Spirit seminar we had attended, walked by me as I was praying. The Lord told me to ask her to wash my feet. I was obedient and I asked her to forgive me for any way that I had hurt her by my indifference during the seminar, and for my attitude that I had toward the Charismatic Renewal. She forgave me and washed my feet. The next day I began to pray in tongues and the other gifts such as healing, words of knowledge, discernment of spirits, etc. became a part of my walk in the Holy Spirit. This same lady became my mentor, especially in the area of deliverance, and she often accompanied us when we were going to deal in that realm. I believe she may have been a very holy woman, as she slowly revealed that for a period of her life she worked closely with the Diocesan exorcist.

Over the years these gifts seemed to fade, and I began to wonder if I were really born again. To make a long story short a friend told me about a tent revival that was coming to the Phoenix area. I decided to attend. During the revival, Todd White had an altar call toward the end of his teaching. I sensed an urge to go forward for the altar call, but felt a bit conflicted because of my Catholic background. As I walked up to the front, I motioned to Todd that I wanted to say something to him, so he leaned over to hear what I had to say. I told him I wanted to know the Jesus that he knew. He seemed to be very moved by my request and repeated what I said into the microphone. Out of the audience a man to come pray with me. When he began to lead me in prayer it was like I became an island unto myself. That is, everything going on around me just faded out of my awareness. When we had finished praying the "sinner's prayer" this man laid hands on me and I fell down under the influence of the Holy Spirit. I have no idea what happened, but when I got up I literally staggered back to my seat. I remember having said things to my friends and their responding with joyful laughter. I have no idea what I had been saying.

The next day, my friends told me there was a prophetic ministry operating outside the main tent and they suggested I go sit under that ministry. My friend's son showed me how to record on my smart phone what was being said. I did just that. The person who seemed to take the lead told me that I had a lot of knowledge of God, not necessarily through reading the Scriptures but that God had been tutoring me over the years. This was true, in that I do not read well and therefore do not read a lot, but all through the years of being healed and in ministering to people God seemed to teach me many things during my prayer time with Him. There were other things that were said which were very encouraging and revealing, but I won't go into them here. However, as I knew we were getting ready to wrap up the session, I became focused on being sure I could stop the recording. Consequently I did not hear the last thing that was said to me. After I left the session I tried to listen to what I had recorded but could not hear it with all the noise around me, so I stopped trying.

I went home that night and went to bed quite tired. When I woke up in the morning around 5:00 A.M., I sat up in bed and shouted "I am a new man." Why I shouted that, I had no idea, especially in light of the fact that I was alone in the house because Anita had gone to Portland Oregon to visit her sister. It was Sunday morning, so I went to our local parish for Mass, and when I got home I wondered if I could e-mail the recording that I had on my phone from the day before. I found that I could indeed do so. After e-mailing it I got on my computer and played the recording. The last thing that was said during the prophecy session the day before, the thing I did not hear, was "You will go to bed tonight and tomorrow you will wake up and you will be a new man." That was mind blowing.

A few weeks after my wife returned from visiting her sister she said to me one day that something had happened to me, that I was like a new man." I told her what had happened and she joked about calling me Newman.

A few months later our oldest daughter stopped by, and when she and I were alone together in the kitchen my daughter said to me, "Dad you are different, you have changed, what happened to you?" I told her about the born again experience and she just said "Wow" in a very joyful way.

Chapter 21

Self Righteousness

I want to briefly talk about self righteousness and how it affects our relationship with God. Here again I am not an expert in this area, so I will talk about my experiences of walking in self righteousness.

A number of years ago, I was attending a presentation by a Catholic lay evangelist by the name of Charlie Osburn. He had another lay evangelist with him, and I believe they were conducting a question and answer session after they had done some teaching. Someone in the audience asked about hearing God speak to them. The question basically was "Do you hear God's voice?" The other evangelist decided to try to answer the question. He started out by asking how many people had ever heard God speak to them. About half the people raised their hands. He then said something that I initially thought was cruel and uncalled for. He basically said that if you are not hearing God speak to you then you are walking in self righteousness. When I prayed about what he had said, I came to realize that whenever I think I am right, it is often very difficult for me to hear another person with regards to the subject.

I also thought about my prayer life and realized that it, for the most part was me telling God what I needed to have done. There was very little, if any, listening to what God wanted. It was during this period, when I knew I needed God's healing, that I started to spend more time in prayer asking God things and listening for an answer.

In the book of James, chapter 1 beginning in verse 5 it tells us:

> ⁵ If any of you lacks wisdom, let him ask God,
> who gives to all men generously and without
> reproaching, and it will be given him. ⁶ But let him
> ask in faith, with no doubting, for he who doubts
> is like a wave of the sea that is driven and tossed
> by the wind. ⁷, ⁸ For that person must not suppose
> that a double-minded man, unstable in all his
> ways, will receive anything from the Lord.

So James tells us that we can ask God for wisdom and he
will give it to us, but we must believe we will receive the
wisdom we asked for.

In chapter 10 of the Gospel of John, we see Jesus talking to
the Jewish leaders:

> ²⁴ So the Jews gathered round him and said to him,
> "How long will you keep us in suspense? If you
> are the Christ, tell us plainly." ²⁵ Jesus answered
> them, *"I told you, and you do not believe. The works
> that I do in my Father's name, they bear witness to me;
> ²⁶ but you do not believe, because you do not belong to
> my sheep. ²⁷ My sheep hear my voice, and I know them,
> and they follow me."*

He tells us His sheep hear his voice, so there are a couple
of questions we have to ask. We need to ask ourselves
questions like, are we trying to lead rather than follow? If
our prayer is predominantly to ask God to do something,
then are we attempting to lead God rather than follow
Him? Sheep don't lead; they are followers of their
shepherd. Or, possibly, is His message too simple for us?
Being religious also tends to make us want to follow rules
rather than follow a shepherd.

When I first started praying for healing for people, I

would ask God to make the next person who came to our house for healing be just like the last person who came. That was so I would know how to pray. I can pretty much tell you that God ignored my request. It became quickly apparent that I had to be led by the Spirit of God when praying for someone to be healed. Putting it simply, I had to learn to rely on God.

When I was trying to put my thoughts together to write this chapter on self righteousness, God reminded me of something that had happened a few years ago. It is a clear example of how walking in self righteousness hinders our ability to really hear the heart of God.

We had decided to celebrate our 50th wedding anniversary by renting a large beach house in San Diego for a week and have all of our children and grandchildren there with us. We had actually spent many summer vacations in San Diego staying near the beach in a tent trailer so it filled us with fond memories for the entire family as our children grew up. While the beach house was on the extravagant side for us, we wanted our 50th to be memorable for all of us. In the weeks that preceded the event I was actually hearing God speak to me to send money to one of our daughters who was evidently in a financial squeeze. While I heard that in my spirit, I was focused on judging how I saw the way she and her husband were making financial decisions. It was not that I knew what was really happening as I was judging from afar, but non-the less, I was passing judgment. So I did not do as God asked me to do. After a few days of wrestling with this, a neighbor came over while we were eating dinner and I began telling the neighbor what I was hearing in my spirit, but that I was reluctant to send any money because of what I believed I had observed. The neighbor told me a very touching story about her daughter, who had died at a relatively young age. She said, "If you have the money, send it to your daughter." I took my neighbor's advice and sent my daughter the money.

When my daughter and her husband arrived at the beach house for the celebration, she took me aside to thank me for the money I had sent. She told me they would not have been able to come had I not sent the money. Can you even begin to imagine the pain for my wife, for myself, for my daughter and her husband, had they not been able to come? And, even for her siblings when they would have learned she was not able to attend the celebration? God's thoughts are far above our thoughts.

When I sat down to write this chapter, God showed me how this had prevented me from hearing the intention of His heart. He showed me how my judging of my daughter and her husband (and like so often is the case, when we judge we really don't even know the entire story) kept me in a condition in which I was ignoring the intention of God's heart. God then told me that He had to send the neighbor over to tell me her story so as to move my heart. Self righteousness is my having to be right in my own mind, and it is a killer of relationships.

This example is a sample of what I was talking about in the previous chapter when the prophetic minister said God "tutored" me.

I think the message is that we must really take a serious look at ourselves and if we judge others, especially if we have trouble hearing God, or if we have never heard God speak to us.

Chapter 22

Sowing Seeds

Another area that needs to be discussed involves sowing, watering and reaping. God sometimes uses us to sow and to water the seeds, but it is God who makes things grow. This comes from 1 Corinthians, chapter 3 verses 1 through 9.

> But I, brethren, could not address you as spiritual men, but as men of the flesh, as babes in Christ. ² I fed you with milk, not solid food; for you were not ready for it; and even yet you are not ready, ³ for you are still of the flesh. For while there is jealousy and strife among you, are you not of the flesh, and behaving like ordinary men? ⁴ For when one says, "I belong to Paul," and another, "I belong to Apollos," are you not merely men? ⁵ What then is Apollos? What is Paul? Servants through whom you believed, as the Lord assigned to each. ⁶ I planted, Apollos watered, but God gave the growth. ⁷ So neither he who plants nor he who waters is anything, but only God who gives the growth. ⁸ He who plants and he who waters are equal, and each shall receive his wages according to his labor. ⁹ For we are God's fellow workers; you are God's field, God's building.

Let's focus on verses 8 and 9. It is important to see those verses in light of the preceding verses. Just like today, with each of us standing behind and defending the theology of our particular denominations, the people then were arguing about who taught them. When we do this, the

Scripture clearly states that we are operating in the flesh. When we operate in the flesh, we clearly are not operating in the Kingdom of God. Thus we have stepped out from under God's power. St Paul is telling us that we need to get out of the flesh and into the spirit because what matters is God's message, not who taught it. The message then is that we are called to be God's fellow workers (verse 9) and as God's workers we are to sow seed and water that seed. Frankly, it does not matter who does the sowing and who does the watering; what matters is that it is God who causes the growth.

I learned most recently that when I view my calling as one who plants or one who waters, when I pray for someone to be healed and healing does not appear to occur right away, I am set free from measuring how I did. Prior to understanding this I tended to be come rather proud (self righteous) when someone got healed; on the other end, I tended to become discouraged when someone did not get healed. This happened because, even though I did not really admit it to myself, I was measuring my "performance" by what transpired. God clearly provides us freedom from this when we understand we are the seed planters and/or those that water the seeds, and that He makes it happen: It is God's job to heal, as I cannot do it. Now I also realize that sometimes a seed needs to be watered more than once before the growth (or healing) reaches maturity.

Here is another point about sowing seeds. The Scriptures tell us in Mark, Chapter 4:

> [30] And he said, "With what can we compare the kingdom of God, or what parable shall we use for it? [31] It is like a grain of mustard seed, which, when sown upon the ground, is the smallest of all the seeds on earth; [32] yet when it is sown it grows up

and becomes the greatest of all shrubs, and puts forth large branches, so that the birds of the air can make nests in its shade."

The smallest seed produces the largest bush which provides shelter for many. So we should avoid measuring the size of the seeds that we sow because we are simply called to sow, and God will take it from there.

Here is an example. We now spend the summers up north away from the Phoenix heat. One day, in the RV Park where we were living, I was walking the dog when I saw a woman moving along very gingerly with a walker. I asked her if she was in pain. Her response was that she had had a hip replacement two days earlier and was in great pain. I asked her if I could pray for her, and took her hand thanking God for His great love for her. I then told the pain to leave her body and told her hip to heal quickly. The next day she told me she slept through the night without any pain. A week after the hip replacement, she replaced her walker with a cane and a week later she walked without any aids. She said she had been pain free from the day I prayed for her. She told me she has since walked four miles in one session. I can tell you that that experience clearly planted a seed, or watered what was already there, not only in her, but in her family as well. She knows God touched her.

Sometimes God commands us to do something by just speaking to us in a particular situation. When God does speak to us we have a choice to listen and do what is asked, or to ignore His voice and not do what He asks. Here is an example of something that happened a few years ago. We were out of town visiting our family. We were at one daughter's house as was our son and his family. My daughter-in-law's sister was also in the area with her two children, so she stopped by to visit her sister before she drove across the state to return home to be with her husband who was working. Just as she was getting ready to leave, I heard God tell me to give her some money. I walked over toward her, reaching into my wallet to get a $20 bill when God said, "no give her $50." I did what I heard and handed her $50 telling her that God wanted her to have this. She was somewhat taken by surprise, but accepted the money with a thank you, and they got into the car and drove off. We went back to Phoenix shortly after that, and a couple of days later my son called to thank me for what I had done. His wife's sister told them that she had very little gas in the car and was too embarrassed to say anything, but she honestly did not know how she was going to get home because she had no money and no credit card to buy gas. Furthermore, she said her husband was not getting paid until the following Friday (this all happened on a Sunday) and they did not have enough food in the house to feed the family that week. The $50 provided all their needs. Needless to say, doing what God asked me to do, namely giving her the money, touched the hearts of a lot of people very deeply, and it certainly planted seeds in a lot of people's hearts. My daughter-in-law comes from a family of eight children and I am quite sure they all heard the story.

This past Christmas season old friends came to town from another state to visit their daughter who lives near us. The wife came over to our house for lunch on Christmas Eve and proceeded to tell us that their oldest daughter was very ill and had just been taken to the hospital. I agreed to visit her daughter that afternoon and pray over her. When I got to the hospital the daughter told me she was unable to walk, she had pneumonia, her heart was operating at an estimated 20% to 40% of its capacity, and her liver was pretty much shot from alcohol consumption. I told her I wanted to pray over her and her response was she did not believe in that kind of prayer. Incidentally, she had been raised Christian and the family had been regular church attendees when she grew up. I told her she didn't have to believe because I believed and that was all that mattered. See Mark 16 versus 15-18. I prayed over her and left the hospital. Christmas morning I heard that she was up and walking, her pneumonia was gone, they believed her liver was functioning properly and her heart was operating at a normal level. They planned to do further tests the next day.

The next day the test proved she was completely healed and she was dismissed from the hospital. Praise God.

In addition to the above, the daughter had severed her relationship with her mother and wanted nothing to do with her. Her mother was, needless to say, heartbroken. They returned to their home in another state, hoping and praying that things would change in the relationship with their daughter.

A few days later the mother called hoping I could give her some advice as to how to make a breakthrough in the broken relationship. I had learned a long time before this that I had no idea how to heal relationships but that God did. I told the mother I would pray and ask God for wisdom. See James 1 verses 5-7. I did so and I heard God tell me that in praying over the daughter for healing on Christmas Eve I had planted the seed and that my part in this was finished. God said he would make the seed grow. I called the mother back and relayed to her what I had heard when I asked God for wisdom. I then told the mother that her part in this was to praise and thank God for what was happening. The fifth chapter of Saint Paul's first letter to the Thessalonians says the following:

[16] Rejoice always, [17] pray constantly, [18] give thanks

in all circumstances; for this is the will of God in Christ Jesus for you.

I told the mother that she was to thank and praise God because she knew that God was tending to her daughter. I also told her God did not need her praise as He already knew He was good, but that praise was for her to take her eyes off the problem and to place her eyes on God.

A week or two later, the mother called to tell me her daughter was back in the hospital with the DTs. She apparently had gone back to drinking. I told her that I would visit her daughter again and proceeded to do so. On the way into the hospital I asked God what I should tell the daughter and I heard, "Tell her the truth."

After talking to the daughter for a few minutes I told her that we all fall short of the mark in how we love each other and I shared my struggles with my mother for much of my life. She told me that she never knew anyone else ever struggled with their relationship with their parents, especially me. I went on to tell her we all need to be reconciled with our parents and that we would never feel whole without it. I told her that she needed to forgive both of her parents for their shortcomings. I then told her she needed to read my book which addressed much of that. She gave me her e-mail address and I sent a draft version of my book to her. Apparently something touched her because her mother called a week or so later to tell me her daughter had called to renew their relationship and was now calling every couple of days. Her mother said that God must have used special fertilizer to make that seed grow so quickly. Praise God.

The world and much of the church needs to experience God's healing power and we have been called to be the instruments to make that happen. Both in Matthew 10 and Luke 10 we are commanded to heal the sick. It is a decision we all have to make. I have found I need to make this decision each and every day. Let's look at Joshua 24 verses 14 and 15.

> [14] "Now therefore fear the LORD, and serve him in sincerity and in faithfulness; put away the gods which your fathers served beyond the River, and in Egypt, and serve the LORD. [15] And if you be unwilling to serve the LORD, choose this day whom you will serve, whether the gods your fathers served in the region beyond the River, or the gods of the Amorites in whose land you dwell; but as for me and my house, we will serve the LORD."

We have made that decision. We will serve the Lord.

Epilogue

Awaken Oh Church and Let Your Light Shine

I thought I was finished writing this book. What is even funnier is that I hadn't even made a real attempt to find a publisher. I had been procrastinating about finding one. I had one set of questions to answer for a publishing company and I was quite intimidated and discouraged by the questions that they want answered. Questions like, "Do you have a TV ministry?" I understand that the publisher would like, as would I, some assurance that what they publish will sell. At the same time in the back of my mind is a theme that was spoken to me by two different prophetic ministries. I chose to sit under the prophetic ministries on two separate occasions, partially out of curiosity and partially looking for direction and encouragement. I mentioned some of the things said to me at one of the prophetic sessions earlier in the book. In both cases, the prophetic word I heard had the same general theme: "Your stuff is going to go around the world" and "You will touch many nations." That encouraged me to get the book wrapped up and published.

A while back I woke up in the middle of the night and I heard God speak to me. I heard God say I was to write about calling the church to AWAKEN AND LET OUR LIGHT SHINE. This must have been similar to what St Francis of Assisi thought when God called him to rebuild the church. My first thought was, "You have to be kidding. Who am I to call the church to wake up?" Then I thought that maybe God keeps adding things to the book as some sort of stimulus to try to get me to move with what I have already written. So I ignored the idea. However, the thought would not go away. One morning I was on the phone with a friend and I told him about what I thought I had heard from God about calling the church to let its light shine. He responded saying that there have been a lot of prophesies calling for the same thing. That caused me to sit and ask God for a word on the subject and I very quickly heard Revelation 3:13.

> [13] He who has an ear let him hear what the Spirit says to the churches.

I thought, "Wow, God is serious. He really does want me to write about the subject." So here goes.

I discovered that in the book of Revelation the wording about "He, who has an ear, let him hear what the Spirit says" is in there a few times. That surely makes it clear that it is important to listen to the Spirit. I wondered why He gave me Revelation 3:13 and not one of the other scriptures that says the exact same thing. So I read on.

In Revelation 3:15- 16 it says:

> [15] "I know your works: you are neither cold nor hot. Would that you were cold or hot! [16] So, because you are lukewarm, and neither cold nor hot, I will spew you out of my mouth."

I don't know what the exact definition of lukewarm is. I know, for me, I don't want to be cold and I surely do not want to be lukewarm. I do want to give some meaning as what it means to be hot for something. The best example I can think of was when I met my wife and fell in love with her. She was always on my mind and I could not be with her enough. I pursued her with all my energy. That, I believe, is being hot. Why does the church need to be hot for God and its light shine? One broad and simple answer is the world is in a mess and man, under his own power, cannot clean it up. I just have to listen to the politicians to know that. The reality is we need God's wisdom and power.

Let's look at John 15.

> I am the true vine, and my Father is the vinedresser. ² Every branch of mine that bears no fruit, he takes away, and every branch that does bear fruit he prunes, that it may bear more fruit. ³ You are already made clean by the word which I have spoken to you. ⁴ Abide in me, and I in you. As the branch cannot bear fruit by itself, unless it abides in the vine, neither can you, unless you abide in me. ⁵ I am the vine, you are the branches. He who abides in me, and I in him, he it is that bears much fruit, for apart from me you can do nothing. ⁶ If a man does not abide in me, he is cast forth as a branch and withers; and the branches are gathered, thrown into the fire and burned. ⁷ If you abide in me, and my words abide in you, ask whatever you will, and it shall be done for you. ⁸ By this my Father is glorified, that you bear much fruit, and so prove to be my disciples. ⁹ As the Father has loved me, so have I loved you; abide in my love. ¹⁰ If you keep my commandments, you will abide in my love, just as I have kept my Father's commandments and abide in his love. ¹¹ These things I have spoken to you, that my joy may be in you, and that your joy may be full.

In the latter part of verse 5 Jesus tells us that apart from Him we can do nothing. So in order to have the power of God we must abide in Him so He can use us to clean up the mess in the world is. To abide means we must remain in Him, we must pursue Him and have Him always on our mind. We do this in prayer. We spend time in the word and we celebrate that with our brothers and sisters when we meet.

Psalm 1, versus 1-3 tells us:

> Blessed is the man who walks not in the counsel of the wicked, nor stands in the way of sinners, nor sits in the seat of scoffers; ²but his delight is in the law of the LORD, and on his law he meditates day and night. ³He is like a tree planted by streams of water, that yields its fruit in its season, and its leaf does not wither. In all that he does, he prospers.

Notice in verse 2 we are told the blessed man meditates on the word day and night (Jesus is the Word made flesh, John 1) and when he does this he is one that produces fruit, he does not whither and he prospers. I believe that meditating on the word day and night helps us to become hot.

Go back to John 15, cited above, and decide for yourself if you are hot or cold or lukewarm.

There are lots of things God promises in the book of Revelation for those who are zealous (hot) for Him and in Revelation 2: He says the following:

> ²⁶He who conquers and who keeps my works until the end, I will give him power over the nations.

Is that victory over the mess the world is in or what? A number of years ago my wife and I attended a retreat focused on marriage. The priest was very much into sports. And he told us if you are playing baseball and you are hitting .333 (you get a base hit once every three official at bats) you are an all star and could be a candidate for the baseball hall of fame. He then said if you are batting .333 with your spouse, you are striking out. God is looking for All Stars and wants us in the Hall of Fame. You can decide where you stand.

In the Gospel of Matthew, chapter 5 verse 1 Jesus tells us:

> [14] "You are the light of the world. A city set on a hill cannot be hid. [15] Nor do men light a lamp and put it under a bushel, but on a stand, and it gives light to all in the house. [16] Let your light so shine before men, that they may see your good works and give glory to your Father who is in heaven."

One thing each and every one of us can do is to let our light shine. It seems to me when we are hot, our light shines more brightly. There are certainly many ways to let our light shine. This book hopefully encourages you to allow healing to be one of the ways for the light to shine. After all, is that not what Jesus did when he walked the earth? He healed the sick and He set the captives free. Before he left to be with the Father he told us to do the same (Luke 10, verse 9).

I want to talk about the clergy's part in this call to wake up and let our light shine. The clergy (ordained) have what I think is a unique part in the body of Christ. I am sure it goes far beyond what I am about to talk about, but this is a decent start and will hopefully do something to help the church to shine more brightly. In Galatians 5 verse 6 Saint Paul tells us:

> [6] For in Christ Jesus neither circumcision nor uncircumcision is of any avail, but faith working through love.

Jesus told us to love our neighbor. So I find I have to pray for a heart like Jesus so I can love as He did. Then maybe the faith I have will work through love. Where does faith come from? I have heard it said that faith is a gift and it is passed on from your mother or father or grandmother. And there may be some truth to that, but let's look and what scripture says.

In the book of Romans chapter 10 versus 14-17 it says the following:

> [14] But how are men to call upon him in whom they have not believed? And how are they to believe in him of whom they have never heard? And how are they to hear without a preacher? [15] And how can men preach unless they are sent? As it is written, "How beautiful are the feet of those who preach good news!" [16] But they have not all obeyed the gospel; for Isaiah says, "Lord, who has believed what he has heard from us?" [17] So faith comes from what is heard, and what is heard comes by the preaching of Christ.

In the book of Titus, chapter 1 versus 1-3 Saint Paul tells the following:

Paul, a servant of God and an apostle of Jesus Christ, to further the faith of God's elect and their knowledge of the truth which accords with godliness, [2] in hope of eternal life which God, who never lies, promised ages ago [3] and at the proper time manifested in his word through the preaching with which I have been entrusted by command of God our Savior.

Notice that he speaks of God's elect, that is us, and that we know God's truth, and that by God's plan it will be manifested in His word through preaching. That pretty much sums up the importance of the preaching of the word.

Our clergy have been sent to preach the word, the good news, and when it is preached the Holy Spirit offers faith to those who listen and believe.

Let me tell you what happened when my wife and I were asked to speak at all our parish masses on sacrificial giving. In doing so, we talked about how we had decided to tithe and included the scriptures that had influenced us to do so. We got a standing ovation at several of the masses. In between the masses our pastor said "You talk about this like you really believe it." My response was that I will only speak about something I believe.

It has been my observation that where the Scriptures are truly preached, calling the people to live them out, that church tends to overflow with attendance. Furthermore, the people appear to be alive in the Lord (I would say more hot than lukewarm or cold) when the word is truly preached. Our people are hungry for the word. In Matthew 4 verse 4, Jesus is in the desert and responds to the devil who is trying to tempt him:

> [4] But he answered, "It is written, 'Man shall not live by bread alone, but by every word that proceeds from the mouth of God.'"

A number of years ago I bought a set of tapes called "Heart to Heart." The tapes were a recording of the last retreat Archbishop Fulton J. Sheen ever gave. He gave the retreat for priests at the largest seminary in Ireland. There were a couple of messages from the retreat that I have never forgotten. The first and foremost was about prayer. While he was speaking to priests this message could apply to every Christian. Bishop Sheen said he spent his entire priesthood praying at least one hour a day (in his case it was before the Blessed Sacrament). He said his entire ability to speak, to minister and to live, in general, flowed from his time with the Lord in prayer. He spent much of the retreat encouraging an hour a day of prayer. I remember he told the priests that if you don't think you have time, then perhaps you should give up something like your cocktail hour in order to pray.

The second subject I remember was the fact that so many in the church were going to school to learn psychological counseling. He was appalled by this. He asked the question, "Whatever happened to the gift of counsel of the Holy Spirit?" He said, "Spend more time with the Lord and you will have all you need to counsel."

I would put Bishop Sheen into the hot category. I want to tell you a story of the effect he had on my mother, who was not of the Catholic faith. In any case, she somehow heard that Bishop Sheen was in town. She asked me to take her to hear him speak. My mother had trouble expressing what she was experiencing but I could tell she had been touched very deeply. Along these same lines, when Mother Teresa came to Phoenix, my father who rarely attended church was glued to the evening news just to catch a glimpse of what she spoke about. That is one of the effects of the Christian who is hot.

What are some of the other reasons we need to be hot?

In the gospel of John in the 17th chapter Jesus prays to the Father that we all be one, so the world may know the Father sent Him.

> 20 "I do not pray for these only, but also for those who believe in me through their word, 21 that they may all be one; even as thou, Father, art in me, and I in thee, that they also may be in us, so that the world may believe that thou hast sent me."

I believe that if Jesus prayed for something then it is

rather important. How is the world going to believe in Jesus when they see a church that is divided? Perhaps the effect of a divided church is easier to see if we look at something like the institution of marriage. If the only marriages we see are ones where the husband and wife were barely talking to each other, where the husband or the wife thinks he/she is right and the other is wrong, it would be pretty hard to believe in marriage. If my wife did not look past my shortcomings and if I did the same with her, there would not be much of a marriage left. The effect is the same when I refuse to see the goodness in people from other denominations and refuse to hear what they have to say.

My wife and I recently attended a day in which people from many denominations attended. The day was under the theme of John 17. There were many wonderful talks. For my Catholic brothers and sisters our bishop gave a moving talk in which he indicated he has heard the call for Christian unity from very early in his priesthood. One of the speakers was Pope Francis via a recorded message. Pope Francis said a couple of things that really struck a chord with me. One was that if you were captured by ISIS they would not ask what church you attended. They would just kill you. The other was that we should not wait for all the theologians to agree before we strive toward unity. He said that our theologians play a great role in helping us relate to God but that he did not think they would all agree until the day after judgment day. We need to become one in Christ to be believable to the world.

We, the church, are in a battle. We need each other. Let me close with two scriptures that I think speak volumes. The first scripture is from Exodus chapter 17.

[8] Then came Amalek and fought with Israel at Rephidim. [9] And Moses said to Joshua, "Choose for

us men, and go out, fight with Amalek; tomorrow I will stand on the top of the hill with the rod of God in my hand." [10] So Joshua did as Moses told him, and fought with Amalek; and Moses, Aaron, and Hur went up to the top of the hill. [11] Whenever Moses held up his hand, Israel prevailed; and whenever he lowered his hand, Amalek prevailed. [12] But Moses' hands grew weary; so they took a stone and put it under him, and he sat upon it, and Aaron and Hur held up his hands, one on one side, and the other on the other side; so his hands were steady until the going down of the sun. [13] And Joshua mowed down Amalek and his people with the edge of the sword.

Notice that Moses went to the hill top to pray for his people involved in the battle. Also notice he took Aaron and Hur with him for support. When Moses was praying, Israel was winning, when he tired and stopped praying Amalek started to prevail. Aaron and Hur provided support for Moses and he remained steady (perhaps we could say hot) with the support and Israel won the battle.

We need each other to stay hot, to pray and to win the battle.

The second scripture is from 2 Chronicles.

[14] If my people who are called by my name humble themselves, and pray and seek my face, and turn from their wicked ways, then I will hear from heaven, and will forgive their sin and heal their land.

That pretty much sums up our call to be hot and to be unified.

AWAKEN OH CHURCH. LET YOUR LIGHT SHINE.

About the Author

Ron and his wife, Anita, have been married over 57 years. They have four children and ten grandchildren. At one time they were coordinators of the southwest for World Wide Marriage Encounter. They then moved into the healing ministry. They have spoken and/or given workshops on the subjects of forgiveness and healing, marriage, family, and parenting at various churches and conventions in the states of Arizona, California, Oregon, Washington, Nevada, Utah, New Mexico and as far east as Ohio.